Grace to be Rich

by
Jay Eberly

JEM Publications

Unless otherwise indicated, all Scripture quotations in this volume are from the *King James Version* of the Bible.

First Printing 1999

0-9669030-0-5

Jay Eberly Ministries
P.O. Box 614
Broken Arrow, OK 74013-0614

Contents

Chapter 1
Vision and Mentality

For ye know the grace of our Lord Jesus Christ, that, though he was rich, yet for your sakes he became poor, that ye through his poverty might be rich.

— 2 Corinthians 8:9

The devil hates it when God's children prosper, and religious people get mad when we talk about money. But the Bible speaks clearly on the subject. It is the will of God that we be rich.

That's good news! Poverty is not our lot in life or our cross to bear, as some of us have been told. God put our poverty on Jesus when He was on the Cross so that we could be rich. What a refreshing relief from the things most of us have heard all our lives. Most of us were discouraged enough about our finances before someone came along telling us God was against us too. But that's what we heard. So we went around with our head down and our shoes and car worn out, thinking we were pleasing the Lord.

What a contrast to what our God is really like! No wonder no one listened to us when we told them about Jesus. But, thank God, some of us have begun to learn the truth of the matter. We found in the Word that we have been given the blessings of Abraham in Christ. We found that

God is a good God, and wants to bless us with material blessings. We have been rising up in our faith ever since and standing for what belongs to us. We have proven His Word to be true time after time. What joy it brings to our hearts to find that God is faithful to His Word.

This book is written to encourage your faith for prosperity. By the time you're through reading it, I trust you will receive a greater revelation of God's goodness toward you in this area. God will truly bless you with good things in this life if you'll renew your mind to the fact that He wants to.

Satan's greatest intention is to blind people's vision of what God really has for them. He'll work overtime to get people to believe anything but the Word of God. The greatest enemy to prosperity is not something natural, but spiritual. You may feel as if you haven't been given the right chances in life or that no one has given you the break you needed, but those aren't the things that hinder people's prosperity. No, the root of poverty is found in the spirit realm. Deceptive little lies that are propagated mostly by the religious teachings of men are what blind many Christians to the will of God for them financially. Religious lies blind and bind people, because they make the Word of God of no effect (Matt. 15:6).

Many good people have allowed religion to tell them what God's character is like. The problem is this: Religion speaks mostly from experiences in this world, where the curse is prevailing, and not from the Bible. Your vision of God will be severely tainted if you are looking through all the smog and fog of Satan's mess down here on the earth. If you and I want to get a clear vision of what our heavenly

Father is like, we must go directly to His Word. I don't mean finding out what someone *else* said God meant; I mean we must know what God actually said!

If God were living on the earth today in any organized society, and if He were doing everything people accuse Him of doing — putting cancer on people, burning houses down, and causing accidents, floods, wars, famines, and babies to be born deformed, and so forth — He would be hanged by ten o'clock tomorrow morning, because we know that sort of thing is wrong! The funny thing is, if the people who say God does bad things to people didn't know that it was God who was being hanged, they would call those who brought Him to justice "good people" for removing such a one from our contact. What I am saying is, they are confused about what is really good and what is evil. The Bible is very plain about the fact that prosperity is good. Prosperity is good, and poverty is not. God isn't confused about it.

Prosperity Is Good, Not Evil

Some will consent that God helps us get by from day to day, all right, but that we really have to be careful about money. "After all, we don't want to get extravagant about it," they say. "We want to keep a balance in this area. You know, there have been people backslide over money."

It all sounds so well-meaning, and I'm sure folks who say this to you are genuinely interested in your well-being. But there's no use taking your doctrine from someone who has backslidden over money. People have drowned in water before because they weren't paying attention to what they were doing, but that doesn't mean I'm never going to have anything to do with water for the rest of my life. It certainly doesn't mean there is anything wrong with water, and I'm not going to let people tell me that there is.

We have to base our doctrine on the Word of God and never on someone else's experience. We must come to recognize the kinds of statements we often hear for what they are. Those false statements are made by people talking out of fear, because their lives aren't based on the Word. If their lives were based on the Word, they wouldn't be spreading fear. They would be talking faith. They have let the devil put the fear of having wealth in them because of what happened to someone else who didn't base his life on the Word. I certainly am not going to base my doctrine on what happened to someone who didn't base his life on the Word.

The truth is, some people you talk to about prosperity will tell you about all the things to be careful of in this area. Anyone who is always down on something isn't in faith in that area, and you shouldn't listen to them. They'll pull you down into the same unbelief they are wallowing in.

God Wants You To Be Rich!

The Word of God has a great deal to say that will inspire your faith for financial abundance. The warnings in this area are never against a financial condition, rather, the Word warns you against a heart condition. In fact, the Bible actually "warns" you ahead of time that you're going to have money and lots of it. Deuteronomy chapter 8 says that *when* we come into all these financial blessings, we are to remember that it was God who gave them to us. By saying "*when* it happens, don't forget me," God is warning us we're going to be rich!

I am becoming more and more convinced as I meditate in the Word that it is God's perfect will for every believer to be flat rich! I don't mean just having enough to get by till the next paycheck — I mean possessing *financial wealth*. I'm talking about financial independence. We have already read Second Corinthians 8:9 that tells us Jesus was made poor that we might be *rich*. There are numerous other verses that tell us the same thing. For example, notice just a few.

PSALM 112:1-3
1 Praise ye the Lord. Blessed is the man that feareth the Lord, that delighteth greatly in his commandments.
2 His seed shall be mighty upon earth: the generation of the upright shall be blessed.
3 WEALTH AND RICHES SHALL BE IN HIS HOUSE: and his righteousness endureth for ever.

PROVERBS 3:9,10
9 Honour the Lord with thy substance, and with the firstfruits of all thine increase:
10 So shall thy barns be FILLED WITH PLENTY, and thy presses shall BURST OUT WITH NEW WINE.

MALACHI 3:10
10 Bring ye all the tithes into the storehouse, that there may be meat in mine house, and prove me now herewith, saith the Lord of hosts, if I will not open you the windows of heaven, and pour you out a bless-

ing, THAT THERE SHALL NOT BE ROOM ENOUGH TO RECEIVE IT.

DEUTERONOMY 28:11-13
11 And the Lord shall make thee PLENTEOUS IN GOODS, in the fruit of thy body, and in the fruit of thy cattle, and in the fruit of thy ground, in the land which the Lord sware unto thy fathers to give thee.
12 The Lord shall open unto thee his good treasure, the heaven to give the rain unto thy land in his season, and to bless all the work of thine hand: and THOU SHALT LEND UNTO MANY NATIONS, AND THOU SHALT NOT BORROW.
13 AND THE LORD SHALL MAKE THEE THE HEAD, AND NOT THE TAIL; AND THOU SHALT BE ABOVE ONLY, AND THOU SHALT NOT BE BENEATH . . . .

2 CORINTHIANS 9:8
8 And God is able to make all grace abound toward you; that ye, ALWAYS HAVING ALL SUFFICIENCY IN ALL THINGS, may abound to every gook work.

ISAIAH 1:19
19 If ye be willing and obedient, ye shall eat the GOOD of the land.

All these verses tell us that it is God's will for us to have a surplus of money. God's name is El Shaddai, not El Cheapo! It's not His will for you to live on just enough to make it by. He wants you to enjoy the best the land has to offer. The first thing that is necessary to appropriate God's best is to renew your mind to this fact.

Many of us have had glimpses of these truths flash across our spirit a time or so, but it's not enough to get a glimpse of God's will for your life. Your spirit man must have the luxury of feasting on the Word concerning *abundance* until it changes your entire inner man. I mean, the Word of God must change your vision and your mentality. *Prosperity doesn't begin with money in your pocket. It begins with the Word finding a home in your heart!* It begins not on the outside of your life, but in your inner life. It begins with a vision of abundance in your heart and a mentality of abundance in your mind.

> **3 JOHN 2**
> **2 Beloved, I wish above all things that thou mayest prosper and be in health, EVEN AS** [relative to, in proportion with, accordingly as] **thy soul prospereth.**

Your soul is your mind, will, and emotions. It is part of your inward man. How does your soul prosper? Some have thought that this is simply referring in a general sense to being born again. Notice verses 3 and 4.

> **3 For I** [John] **rejoiced greatly, when the brethren came and testified of THE TRUTH THAT IS IN THEE, even as THOU WALKEST IN THE TRUTH.**
> **4 I have no greater joy than to hear that my children WALK IN TRUTH.**

The apostle John is telling Gaius that the truth of the Word was prospering his soul. That's not something that happens automatically when you're born again. This is called renewing the mind with the Word of God (Rom. 12:2).

Just because you think every now and then about the fact that God wants you to be rich, doesn't mean that your mind is renewed. Ephesians 4:23 says, *"And be renewed in the SPIRIT OF YOUR MIND."* You can sit and hear someone teach that God wants to bless you financially, and the spirit of your mind (your mental inclination) not be renewed. The goal of renewing your mind is not reached until the Word of God changes your *mentality*.

A thought doesn't constitute a mentality. *Many* thoughts constitute a mentality! Mentality is a mode or way of thinking. It is one's mindset, outlook, or mental inclination. It is one's prevailing tendency to think in a particular way. It is the rut that one's mind goes to when there are no preachers or faith people around.

Many people can hear the message of prosperity and even shout and say amen, but because of a deep "poverty" rut in their thinking, they slide back into their old mentality during the week. They'll go to lunch after the service and criticize the pastor's wife for her expensive shoes. They need to meditate in the Word until they form a Bible rut. Only then will things begin to change for the better financially.

Wrong Thinking About God Will Hinder Your Prosperity

If you think wrongly about God, it will make you miss Him by a hundred miles. We all like to think that God thinks the way we do about everything. For example, you might see someone spend more money than you would on some piece of "unnecessary" merchandise and judge them in your heart for spending too much money. *They already have one pair of shoes almost like that*, you may think.

But just because you think that way doesn't mean God does. The truth is, God would probably have thirty-three hundred pairs. And those are just the red pairs! God is a rich God, and He does everything very extravagantly. He can't help Himself — that's just the way He is.

When God made the birds, He could have made two colors of birds, and that would have been enough. When He made dogs, two kinds of dog would have been enough, wouldn't it? Why did He make all the different colors and shapes of flowers? We don't need all of them, do we? No! No one said we did! God said in Genesis 2:9 that He made them because they are pretty to look at. He didn't make them because we *needed* them. He's just a God who likes to enjoy things, and He made us the same way. He doesn't just give us things when we need them. He is an extravagant God who is excessive in everything He does. The only way you and I are going to develop the capacity to receive excess as He has is to meditate in His Word until we begin to think as He does.

God Is Not 'Balanced'!

The city God lives in is solid gold, and it's no small place either. It's fifteen hundred miles long, fifteen hundred miles wide, and fifteen hundred miles high (*see* Revelation 21:12-17). That's a lot of gold, and it's His perfect will for you to live there. Not just now and then, but for eternity. That's the way God thinks about prosperity. He is totally unbalanced about the subject of prosperity. He doesn't believe in "a little bit of poverty and a little prosperity," as some might put it, to keep one balanced. Jesus bore your poverty, that you might be rich right down here on the earth.

The whole context of Second Corinthians 8 and 9 is financial riches down here in this life. Therefore, Jesus became poor that we might be totally rich — not that we might have a little poverty and a little prosperity to keep us from getting unbalanced on the subject. He's talking about being extremely rich all the time! He's not "balanced" on anything that is His will. It's His will that we live free from sin. He's not balanced on the subject. In other words, He doesn't believe in a little sin here and there to keep from getting out of balance on the subject. He believes in living right all the time. We know He does because *He* lives right all the time.

The same is true concerning health and healing. It's His perfect will that we live our full lives out in divine health — not having a little sickness now and then to teach us something or to keep us balanced on the subject. Our Father believes in being healthy all the time. We know He does because *He's* healthy all the time.

The same is true concerning His will for us to prosper. He's not balanced on the subject. He doesn't believe in a little poverty now and then to keep us humble, or to keep a balance on the subject. Our Father believes in being rich all the time. We know He does because He's rich all the time.

I've heard people say, "Well, I know God doesn't *mind* if we have money." Once again, a statement such as that reveals that one's mind hasn't been renewed with the Word of God yet. They still think religiously about God's will to prosper us. If you want to get different results than most everybody else is getting, then you're going to have to think differently than most everybody else thinks.

The Bible never said that God doesn't mind if we have money. It says that He has *pleasure* in the prosperity of His servants (Psalm 35:27). There is a big difference! We don't tell people, "God doesn't *mind* if you get saved," do we? Why? Because His will isn't passive in the matter. When people say God doesn't mind if you have money, they are saying it as if prosperity is His acceptable or permissive will. God's will is never passive like that. It's filled with determination.

In Mark 1:40-42, a blind man came to Jesus and said, "*. . . If thou wilt, thou canst make me clean.*" Jesus put His hand on him and said, "*I will, be thou clean.*" The Bible says that as soon as Jesus spoke those words, the man's leprosy left him. The words "I will" in the Greek mean *I am determined, I am delighted, I am resolved,* and *I have pleasure in doing it.* In other words, the will of God is not a passive thing. When we find God's will in His Word, we find something that God is determined to do for us. As far as He is concerned, prosperity is not a side issue. How could it be when He purchased it with the blood of Jesus?

As long as people believe, "God doesn't mind if we have money," they're not in agreement with God. If God's will isn't passive, then our faith ought not be passive. We'll have to have the same attitude that God has about prosperity if we're going to experience the perfect will of God in the area of prosperity. We'll have to have a spirit of faith (2 Cor. 4:13) and not a spirit of passivity or apathy.

Most people just pick up their mentality from everyone around them, rather than from the Bible. Their mentality is formed by teachings, environment, and associations. When it comes to most churches, you'll not get the right mentality from any of these three. The most passive, poverty-minded people you'll ever meet are in church! If you associate with them, you're going to pick up a mentality that will keep you broke.

Mark this down and don't forget it: Until you get a prosperous mentality from the Word, you'll never have a spirit of faith come on you in the area of prosperity, and you'll never live above the devil's junk and lies.

Many fine Christian people have picked up a poverty spirit from those around them. I don't mean that these Christians are demon-possessed. There is no such thing as a born-again believer being demon-possessed, because believers are the temple of the Holy Spirit. A demon possessed person has been taken over by an evil spirit — spirit, soul, and body. A demon can't take over a Christian's spirit, because the Greater One lives in him (1 John 4:4).

However, there are various degrees or levels of demon activity. You need to know that! All demon activity is not demon possession. Demons will take as much ground as a person will yield to them, even though he or she may be a Christian and has the authority to resist them. Many times demons begin to work on people through their thought life. When I say that some people have a poverty spirit, I mean they have yielded to thoughts of poverty to the point the devil has taken over their thought life in that area. Their thoughts are locked up to the point they can't think anything but poverty thoughts or say anything but, "We can't afford that" or "That's too expensive."

When ministers teach, "God doesn't *mind* if you have

money," they are actually helping the devil bind up the minds of their people, because, as I said, the Bible never said that God doesn't mind if we have money. It said God *delights* in the prosperity of His people! When people see the roof of their church building leaking, the paint peeling, and the pew covers wearing away, the environment itself is giving them a poverty spirit, especially when the congregation believes that God *wants* it that way. When they see the pastor wearing old suits and outdated ties and driving a rust-bucket car to church, they're going to get a mentality about how God pays His ministers. If God calls their children into the ministry, they won't want anything to do with it!

The Outward Experience Follows The Inward Revelation

Most Christians just don't have prosperity on the inside of them yet. If you're going to believe God for abundance, you're going to have to have it on the inside first. Faith has the inward experience before it has the outward experience. If your spirit man has not yet been consumed with the Word of God along this line, Satan will easily steal the outward experience of prosperity away from you.

Everything God does in man, He does from the inside out. The New Birth gave you a righteous nature in your spirit man. Only then could you put a stop to the unrighteous acts of sin in your flesh. Divine healing works the same way. God heals man's body through his spirit. The healing seed of the Word must enter man's spirit first, and then healing comes to the physical body. Many have tried to bypass that step and go directly to the healing in the physical body.

Without the manifestation of one of the gifts of the Spirit, it won't work that way. The seed of divine healing must first register on a man's spirit before healing can come to the body (Prov. 4:20-23).

The same is true concerning divine prosperity. Prosperity that comes from God begins in the spirit of man and works its way out into his life's experience. Proverbs 23:7 says, *"...As he thinketh IN HIS HEART, so is he...."* According to this verse, the way a man thinks in his heart has a lot to do with what he is or what he becomes in life. Nowhere is this more evident than in the lives of children. Most children never rise above what their parents tell them as they are growing up. The words that are planted in their heart form their inner identity, and their inner man will bring forth accordingly.

Notice this principle in Joshua 1:8. *"THIS BOOK OF THE LAW shall not depart out of thy mouth; but thou shalt meditate therein day and night, that thou mayest OBSERVE TO DO according to all that is written therein: for THEN THOU SHALT MAKE THY WAY PROSPEROUS, and then thou shalt have good success."* Notice that this verse starts out with the Word of God (the seed) and ends up with prosperity. Once again, the reason is that the Word is the source of divine prosperity. Oh, people may get money some other way, but that doesn't really make it prosperity, nor is it divine. We're talking about the *"... blessing of God that maketh rich, and addeth no sorrow with it"* (Prov. 10:22).

That came to me as a great revelation back a few years ago when I was struggling to find some answers for my own life financially. The thing that began to set me free was the revelation that prosperity begins with the Word of God, not with more money coming into my hands. So many times we want to get the cart before the horse, so to speak. We want the end result, but somehow miss the thing that brings those results. Some have heard the testimony of others who received a financial blessing from the Lord, but only heard *what* happened and not *how* it happened.

If you will learn God's ways, you can enjoy the same results over and over again. The Indians used to say, "Give a man a fish,and he'll eat for a day — teach a man to fish, and he'll eat for a lifetime." God wants to teach us how to prosper, rather than just hand us money.

Prosperity Begins With a Vision

Prosperity begins with a vision on the inside, and the Word is the source of that vision. You must see yourself prosperous before you become prosperous. You've got to be able to see yourself paying things off. You've got to see yourself giving thousands of dollars. If you can't see yourself prospering and get excited about it, then you can't go there. You have to observe it before you can have it.

A passage of Scripture that has helped my wife and me along this line is First Kings chapter 4. It speaks of King Solomon's wealth. Verses 21-28 speak of his daily table settings. He and those at his table ate 270 bushels of flour a day, 540 bushels of meal (probably made into bread and cakes, etc.), 30 oxen, 100 sheep, plus a multitude of deer, harts, and fatted fowl. Verses 26-28 tell us that he had 40,000 stalls for horses and 12,000 horsemen. That certainly is abundance, isn't it? Some would have a problem with King Solomon if he were alive today, especially if he lived in their town and went to their church. They would be offended at all his wealth.

But that just shows why they aren't enjoying it themselves. They don't have the capacity to receive that kind of wealth, or they wouldn't be so offended at it. The reason Solomon was able to receive all this wealth was because he had the capacity of heart to receive it. Verse 29 of First Kings 4 says, *"And God gave Solomon wisdom and understanding exceeding much, AND LARGENESS OF HEART, even as the sand that is on the sea shore."*

In order to receive greater things from the Lord, you must have your heart enlarged. It's not enough to desire big things. Some people have never even desired to enjoy big things like that. But even if you do, desire isn't enough. You must have the capacity of heart to be able to receive them by faith.

There is a great difference between desiring something, and being able to believe God for it. In order to believe God for something, you must have the capacity of spirit to receive it and the strength of spirit to grasp it and bring it to yourself. Desire never gets any kind of a grip on the blessings of God. Of course, if you don't even desire to be rich, you won't believe for it. Mark 11:24 tells us that desire comes before faith.

The 'Barely-Get-By' Mentality Offends God

I've heard people say, "Well, Brother Jay, I really don't want many things from the Lord like that. You know, I'm happy as long as I have enough to get by." One day someone said that to me, and it started bothering me on the inside. Later, when I was alone, I asked the Lord about it. He said, "They have no idea how good I am and how much I want to give it to them, or they wouldn't say that." You know, that's true. It must hurt the Lord for us to reject His love. We've already seen that He has pleasure in our prosperity.

"Well, now, Brother Jay, money can't make you happy, though." When people say that, the first thing I think is, poverty can't make you happy either! Besides, we're not talking about receiving things to make us happy; we're talking about letting God bless us as He wants to so He'll be happy. It glorifies God for us to receive what He has made available to us. Doesn't it bless you to give things to your children? On the other hand, let's not get religious about enjoying things. If God has pleasure in your prosperity, what's wrong with *your* having pleasure in your prosperity. First Timothy 6:17 tells us that God gives us richly all things to enjoy. I think we need to barbecue a sacred cow in this area!

The person who said, "Money can't make you happy" didn't get that kind of thinking out of the Bible. I've never seen that statement in the Bible, have you? Those kinds of statements have come out of a religious tradition and were probably started by someone who was poor. The devil fed someone that line in order to make him feel better in his defeated condition and to keep him from believing God for riches.

The statement "Money can't make you happy" sounds so good, but it is actually old, ugly, unbelief dressed up in a pretty wrapper. Why do I say that? Notice this passage.

PSALM 144: 13-15
13 That our garners [barns] **may be full, affording all manner of store: that our sheep may bring forth thousands and ten thousands in our streets:**
14 That our oxen may be strong to labour, that there be no breaking in, nor going out; that there be no complaining in our streets.
15 HAPPY IS THAT PEOPLE, THAT IS IN SUCH A CASE: YEA, HAPPY IS THAT PEOPLE, WHOSE GOD IS THE LORD.

God said when your accounts are full and your business is multiplying, it makes you happy. The person who said, "Money can't make you happy" has never had any money, or else his God isn't the Lord. Psalm 144:15 said if God is your Lord, and you have money, it makes you happy. That's a revelation if you'll grab hold of it. The only way money can make you happy is when Jesus is your Lord, because He enables you to be rich and be free from your money at the same time. It's only when you're free from money that you can enjoy it. When people say money can't make you happy, they are talking about having money without Jesus.

We need to be careful not to apply the things the Bible says about the ungodly to the believer. Proverbs 10:22 says, *"The blessing of the Lord, it maketh rich, AND HE ADDETH NO SORROW WITH IT."* When money comes through God's blessing, there's no sorrow with it. That means "The blessing of the Lord" will make you happy. Jesus said in John 16:24, *"Hitherto have ye asked nothing in my name: ask, and ye shall receive, that your joy may be full."*

You Will Serve God or Money, But You Can't Serve God *and* Money

One of two things is going to happen in your life. Either Jesus will be your master, or else money will make you its slave. If you aren't serving Jesus, you'll be serving money. Luke 16:13 says, "*No servant can serve two masters: for either he will hate the one, and love the other; or else he will hold to the one, and despise the other. Ye cannot serve God and mammon.*"

What Jesus is telling us is that you can't serve both Him and money at the same time. He didn't say you can't *have* both; He said you can't *serve* both. Nor did Jesus say you can't serve God *with* your money. One of the best ways I know to enjoy your day to the fullest is to find someone to give something to. That's living. That's the abundant life. That's the good life.

Jesus said in Luke 12:15 (*NEB*), "*Beware! Be on your guard against greed of any kind, for even when a man has more than enough, his wealth does not give him life.*"

We need to know that if we live only to get things, we'll never enjoy life. But, then, people who exist just for money aren't making Jesus the Lord of their lives, either.

A person who is living just to get more money is called a fool (Prov. 1:32), and his foolishness will destroy him. We have a parable in Luke 12, right after Jesus told us not to exist only to acquire things, which further explains what Jesus was talking about.

LUKE 12:16-21
16 And he spake a parable unto them, saying, The ground of a certain rich man brought forth plentifully:

17 And he thought within himself, saying, What shall I do, because I have no room where to bestow my fruits?
18 And he said, This I will do: I will pull down my barns, and build greater; and there will I bestow all my fruits and my goods.
19 And I will say to my soul, Soul, thou hast much goods laid up for many years; take thine ease, eat, drink, and be merry.
20 But God said unto him, Thou fool, this night thy soul shall be required of thee: then whose shall these things be which thou hast provided?
21 So is he that layeth up treasure for himself, AND IS NOT RICH TOWARD GOD.

It wasn't that this rich man became more wealthy. Rather, it was that he thought his money was going to give him the good life. It was the fact that he wasn't rich toward God. Money doesn't buy you the good life; *giving* does. Gain isn't godliness (1 Tim. 6:5). Giving is godliness, and godliness is gain (3 John 6). You may have to think about those statements for a moment, but as soon as you get the revelation of them, you'll be much wiser than most church people.

We need to serve the Lord and make money serve us. Money is a wonderful tool, but a harsh master. Don't allow it to rule your life. Make it obey you.

Galatians 6:8 tells us, "*For he that soweth to his flesh shall of the flesh reap corruption; but he that soweth to the Spirit shall of the Spirit reap life everlasting.*" This verse tells us that if we sow to the Spirit (give into something that the Spirit is doing), we will reap everlasting life. That is the "God kind of life." We might call it the good life or life to the fullest. It's a life as God has. It is joy, peace, health, freedom from fear, abundance, and on and on.

My point is, when people say money can't make you happy, they are applying something the Bible says about the unbeliever to the believer.

The Lord wants us to receive His goodness. It glorifies Him for us to be blessed big like Solomon. God wants to be properly represented in the earth. When we won't receive what He wants to do for us, it causes others to see God wrong. God wants to make you an illustration of His goodness for all to see. It is His goodness that leads men to repentance. Most people will never receive a vision of abundance from the Word. Many will have to see God's Word working in you first. For that reason, God wants to make you a living epistle, known and read of all men.

So get a vision for abundance! How does it come? It comes from meditating on the Scriptures along this line. Satan will fight you. He wants to show you a vision of poverty and lack and of things staying as they've always been. He certainly doesn't want you to see that God really does want you blessed. He knows that if he can keep you in the dark about divine prosperity, you will never be able to receive it. But if you'll listen to the Holy Ghost, He will show you the Father. It's not just His job to *tell* you about the Father; rather, it is the Holy Spirit's job to show you the Father in your heart.

One of the greatest things about God is His ability to "show" you what He says to you. What do I mean? I mean He is able to cause you to "see" what He is saying. I think this has been something people have missed in their faith life. They have thought that when your heart believes the Word, it is just sort of a dead thing, such as when you believe in the natural that the earth is round. There is a difference.

The Word of God Is a Living Substance With the Power To Change You!

The Word of God is alive; therefore, when you hear God speak, it is a living thing. When you hear God speak, He not only speaks, but He shows it to you in your spirit. You will say something such as, "Oh, I see what pastor has been trying to say for the last three years. He's been trying to say that God wants to make us rich...," and you'll go on and on repeating what your pastor has been preaching for the past three years.

Up until then it was just a dead message to you, but you heard the prosperity Word long enough until God spoke it to your spirit, and *showed* you what your pastor had been saying. Thank God, you honored the Word enough to keep hearing it. The interesting thing is that it's not until people see God's Word or get a revelation of His Word that things will begin to change for the better in their lives. Let's look at some scriptures along this line.

PSALM 119:130
130 THE ENTRANCE OF THY WORDS GIVETH LIGHT [it takes light to see]; **it giveth understanding unto the simple.**

PSALM 19:8
8 The statutes of the Lord are right, rejoicing the heart [You get happy about God's Word when you see it!]: **the commandment of the Lord is pure ENLIGHTENING THE EYES.**

PSALM 89:19
19 THEN THOU SPAKEST IN VISION to thy holy one [when the Lord spoke, this man saw it]**, and saidst, I have laid help upon one that is mighty; I have exalted one chosen out of the people.**

ISAIAH 22:14
14 And it was REVEALED [Hebrew: uncovered, disclosed, shown, denuded] **IN MINE EARS by the Lord of Hosts....**

JEREMIAH 2:31
31 Oh generation, SEE YE THE WORD OF THE LORD....

JAMES 1:23,25
23 For if any be a HEARER OF THE WORD, and not a doer, HE IS LIKE UNTO A MAN BEHOLDING his natural face in a glass....
25 But whoso LOOKETH into the perfect law of liberty, and continueth therein, he being not a forgetful HEARER, but a doer of the work, this man shall be blessed in his deed.

PROVERBS 29:18
18 Where there is no VISION [Hebrew: seeing, revelation]**, the people perish....**

The reason getting a vision is such a key to victory is because it's such a key to faith. Vision is simply what you see in your heart. You must see the Word before you can believe it. In one sense of the word, you could say that "seeing is believing." What do I mean?

2 CORINTHIANS 4:18
18 WHILE WE LOOK not at the things which are seen, but AT THE THINGS WHICH ARE NOT SEEN: for the things which are seen are temporal; BUT THE THINGS WHICH ARE NOT SEEN [which we look at] **are eternal.**

2 CORINTHIANS 5:7
7 For we walk by faith, not by sight.

The Apostle Paul is telling us that in order to believe something, we have to see it. Now that may sound strange to the casual reader, but I'm talking about one's spiritual eyes being opened to the reality of what God is saying. I'm talking about seeing things that are not seen! If you can't *see* in your heart that Jesus made you rich, then you can't *believe* that Jesus made you rich. You have to see it when you hear it in order to believe it. If all you see in your heart is yourself staying in the same old place financially, then you'll not overcome poverty.

It's one thing for a person to be having financial problems, but it's another thing entirely for those problems to get inside of them. That's when you've been overcome by the enemy. Did you notice that it's "the entrance of his word that giveth light" (Ps. 119:130). The Word has to find entrance into your inner man before you see yourself overcoming poverty. The same is true with the devil's vision of defeat that he tries so hard to get into you. As long as defeat doesn't "enter in" (Mark 4:19) you've still got the victory, no matter what is going on in your bank account. Glory to God!

Identify With the Revelation, Not the Situation

The way you see something greatly affects your response to circumstances, tests, and trials. When you see yourself prosperous through the blood of Jesus, you'll just laugh at lack when it comes. You are identifying with the revelation, not the situation. If you are identifying with circumstances, you'll give in to poverty's intimidation (even though it is powerless against you), simply because you see it as reality. But if you meditate on the Word, it will become more of a reality in your spirit than the circumstances you are facing.

I remember a man telling me once that he had a job driving dump trucks. He got up early every morning and drove the truck to the work site. On one particular morning, he was driving along a quiet country road just as the sun was coming up. The shadows were long and funny looking. At one point, he saw a large black object lying right in his lane of traffic, and he swerved hard just in time to get out of the way. As he flew around the object, he glanced down to see what it was and realized that he had just dodged the shadow of a large sign along the road!

I think that's what a lot of Christians are doing. The devil has them seeing things. They're shadow-dodging. The curse of poverty is everywhere on this earth, and that curse will cast a shadow on your road to prosperity.

The Psalmist David called this earth walk a walk through "*. . . the valley of THE SHADOW of death. . .*" (Ps. 23:4). The curse is all around us, but don't let the shadows that it may cast on you frighten you. Shadows just make things look bad when they're really not. If Jesus was made poor that you might be rich, then you're rich even when things look bad. Don't let the devil show you things that have no substance to them, and don't let him get you to act as if they are real. Your faith in his shadow will create a reality. Meditate on the Word until God's light strikes your spirit and dispels the devil's shadows. When the prosperity scriptures become more real to you than the devil's shadows, then your faith will give substance to prosperity.

Don't be like the ten spies who saw themselves as grasshoppers and said that the Canaanites also saw them as grasshoppers (Num. 13:33). That was the devil showing them a vision of defeat. When you're a spy, you don't go out and ask the enemy, "How do you see us compared to you?" They were letting the devil tell them how little they were compared to the giants. The ten spies said that the enemy saw them as grasshoppers because that's how they saw themselves.

They should never have compared themselves to those giants. Rather, they should have compared those giants to God, like David did when he met Goliath. David never called Goliath a giant. He called him an uncircumcised Philistine, who was no match for a man who had a covenant with God Almighty (1 Sam. 17:36,37)! David had a vision of victory and a positive mentality based on the Word of God.

Chapter 2
How Much Is Enough?

God is very extravagant. If you don't believe it, all you have to do is look around and notice all the different kinds of animals and birds there are. If you or I had made them, we wouldn't have made even a tenth of what He did!

I was recently in Florida ministering, and someone told me that there are over one hundred and twenty different kinds of palm trees. I thought to myself, *That sounds just like God.* One variety just isn't enough for Him. He has to make over a hundred varieties of just one kind of tree! Now some of you men know where your wife gets it when she wants another pair of shoes that look almost like the pair she bought last month!

Now I know that some people don't like this kind of preaching, but I've observed that those are the people who are usually having problems financially as well. Any area of the Word of God that you get offended at will be the area that your faith won't work because offense will steal it from you. There is no such thing as being offended and being in faith at the same time. If you love the Word, you won't be offended at it (Ps. 119:165).

Does Wealth Bother You?

You can really tell where your faith is in this area by determining at what point wealth starts to bother you.

Certainly, people can go about obtaining wealth the wrong way and not use it to bless others. But that doesn't mean that having money in and of itself is evil or that everyone who has money obtained it the wrong way. If we go about obtaining money the way the Lord has instructed us, we'll become very rich, and all our priorities will be in the right place, and we'll be a great blessing to others.

Never in His Word has the Lord ever rebuked someone for receiving something that He had for them, even if it was much more than they needed. We need to get past the idea that the Lord will correct someone for receiving or having more than they need. We owe no apologies to anyone for the blessings of God. Apologizing for what God gave you is false humility, and it is displeasing to the Lord. It also reveals that you don't know God very well in this area. God commanded His people in the Old Testament to rejoice in all His blessings. He said that if they didn't, it would open the door for the curse to come back on them.

DEUTERONOMY 28:47,48
47 Because thou servedst not the Lord thy God WITH JOYFULNESS, AND WITH GLADNESS OF HEART, FOR THE ABUNDANCE OF ALL THINGS;
48 Therefore shalt thou serve thine enemies which the Lord shall send against thee, IN HUNGER, AND IN THIRST, AND IN NAKEDNESS, AND IN WANT OF ALL THINGS: and he [the enemy] **shall put a yoke of iron upon thy neck, until he have destroyed thee.**

Most people don't know God very well in this way. They still haven't understood the fact that He wants them to be rich and to enjoy prosperity (1 Tim. 6:17). They are still letting the devil tell them that God would be displeased with them in some way if they were. Until you lay aside condemnation in this area and receive abundance from God, you're not really even in position to please Him fully — even in your giving.

What do I mean when I say you can't please God when you're under condemnation in the area of prosperity? First, Jesus came to set you free from condemnation (Rom. 8:1), and He has made you worthy to receive all of God's blessings (Col. 1:12).

Second, God said that He has pleasure in the prosperity of His servants (Ps. 35:27). We know from Hebrews 11:6 that without faith, it is impossible to please Him, so Psalm 35:27 is telling us that when we use our faith and receive the blessing of prosperity, it pleases the Lord.

If you are under condemnation for having or enjoying nice things, you are listening to the devil. Condemnation and faith are never found in the same place together. If you are giving out of condemnation, it won't please God, either, because faith is what pleases Him (Heb. 11:6).

God wants you to have more than enough so that you can give, but the first reason He wants to bless you with more than enough is because of His love for you. That's just the way He is. He is so much that way that one of His names is El Shaddai (Gen. 17:1).

I believe the Body of Christ has used giving as an *excuse* to prosper. It's God's perfect will that you have more than you really need because, first of all, He loves you. Now I know that may bother some people, but we need to get this straight in our thinking, or we'll be motivated by condemnation to give.

I meet people all across the nation who are under condemnation in their giving. They have learned how to step out and give — even to the point of sacrifice — but they don't know how to enjoy anything. Someone needs to stand up and set these people free from condemnation. Yes, we need to sow big seeds, but we shouldn't do it because we've been put under condemnation by some preacher to do it. That's not being motivated by faith to give, and it won't please the Lord no matter how much you "shovel" into the offering plate!

I think some preachers have the idea that if we preach that the first reason God wants to bless us is that He loves us and has made a covenant of prosperity with us, people will become covetous and selfish, and won't give. Actually, just the opposite is true, because the knowledge of God's love will set people's faith free. They'll give more freely because they know how good He is and how easy it is to receive from Him! Besides, if people are giving out of condemnation, they aren't going to get blessed for it, anyway, because it takes *faith* to please God.

God Wants To Establish His Covenant With *You*!

I think we have missed something in Deuteronomy 8:18 along this line. Let's look at it again. *"But thou shalt remember the Lord thy God: for it is he that giveth thee power to get wealth,* THAT HE MAY ESTABLISH HIS COVENANT *which he sware unto thy fathers, as it is this day."*

We often pull out the part that says, "*. . . that he may establish his covenant . . .*" and translate it to mean the spreading of the Gospel. Certainly, that is included, but that isn't exactly what this verse said. If you look up the word "establish" in the original language it means *to confirm* or *to make good on a promise*. In other words, God said that He was giving us power to get wealth because He had said that He would.

God doesn't just give us things because He wants us to give them all away, any more than you give your children things just because you want them to give them all away. You are pleased when they do give things away, but you give things to them to bless *them* first of all. So, let's get past all the condemnation for having abundance. He wants us to have extra.

I like the way a verse in the Old Testament reads. *"The liberal soul shall be made fat: and he that watereth shall be watered also himself"* (Prov. 11:25). We all know what fat is — it's extra. It's something that we could live without. From the context of this verse, we know He means that we will be made fat financially. God never said that He would just get us by financially so that we have just enough. He said He would make us *fat*. That means fat bank accounts. Maybe someone you know has condemned you for having something you didn't really need, but God won't. He said He'll give you more than enough. And He won't condemn you for it; He *delights* in it!

To God it's not a luxury to have more than you need, because He's used to having an abundant supply. In fact, He has never known anything else. When you have more than you need, He doesn't think you're being extravagant, because to Him more than enough is just normal. To Him, it's unusual *not* to have a lot of wealth. In fact, He's got so much, He's not even used to thinking about it. The only reason we think about money is, we need to be sure not to overspend. But God has so much, He doesn't need to think about it.

We need to realize this fact, because we need to know God's attitude toward answering our prayers along this line. It's not an issue to Him of "Do you really need it?" He doesn't operate on the basis of need. In fact, the only thing He listens for when you come asking for something is His own Word. He's not waiting to hear you say you need something. He's waiting to hear you say, "Lord, You said such-and-such in Your Word. You made a covenant with me and guaranteed it with the blood of Jesus, and I know You don't lie."

Become Covenant-Conscious, Not Need-Conscious

You may not even *need* a particular thing, but He'll still give you what you ask for, because He made a covenant with you of "more than enough." We are so need-conscious, but we need to become covenant-conscious and God-conscious. If we become caught up in His Word and His way of thinking, we'll begin to receive beyond our needs.

In other words, we'll get to the place that enough is not enough unless it's too much! That's the way God is! He can't help Himself; He's just a God of too much. When He fills us with joy, it's unspeakable (1 Peter 1:8). When He ministers His peace to us, it passes our understanding (Phil. 4:7). He told us to drink of His Spirit to the point of excess and drunkenness (Eph. 5:18). He's just an "*. . . exceeding abundantly above all we can ask or think. . .*" (Eph. 3:20) kind of God! He doesn't believe in just getting by; He believes in having life and that more abundantly.

JOHN 10:10
10 The thief [the devil] **cometh not, but for to steal, and to kill, and to destroy: I** [Jesus] **am come that they might have life, and that they might have it MORE ABUNDANTLY.**

"More abundantly" in the Greek means *excessively, beyond abundant*, *superabundant*, and *exceedingly abundantly above abundant*. I like that, don't you? God is very excessive! He thinks way beyond what we do. When someone says "water," we think of a glass full of water. God thinks of every cloud in the sky, as well as every puddle, creek, stream, river, lake, and ocean — all at the same time!

Be Careful How You Hear

We need to realize that we are constantly measuring everything we hear by the way we're used to thinking. Mark 4:24 says, "*...Take heed what ye hear: with what* *measure ye mete, it shall be measured to you: and unto you that hear shall more be given.*" Jesus is telling us to incline our ears to hear only the Word, but He is also telling us that once our ears are inclined to hear the Word, we should be careful *how* we hear the Word. He is saying that we determine the measure of blessings we receive from the Word by *how* we hear the Word.

Just a few verses earlier Jesus had given the parable of the sower and said that the good ground brought forth fruit "*. . . some thirtyfold, some sixty, and some an hundred*" (Mark 4:20). In other words, He is telling us that the way we hear the Word determines if we get a thirty-, sixty-, or hundredfold blessing. You or I may be good ground but still not be receiving the full blessing from the Word that is available, because we are measuring what the Word says by our own thinking.

When the Word tells us that Jesus was made poor that we might be rich, people measure "rich" many different ways. Some think of getting caught up on their current bills, some think of having more money than bills every month, and some think of paying their creditors off. God will meet each person at his point of faith, but, the truth is, when you study the Bible, none of these people are thinking "rich" yet.

If we take the whole counsel of God on the subject, rich not only means having enough to pay cash for everything without going to the bank, it means you *are* the bank! In other words, Deuteronomy chapter 28 says that we would lend and not borrow. If you are lending, you are the bank!

When you understand the will of God in this area, you realize that God is telling us that we can be independently wealthy. That means that by His grace, we are able to do anything we want or need to do at any time for anybody (2 Cor. 9:8).

The Body of Christ needs to get more of a mentality like He has. When we do, we'll begin to preach the Gospel to the whole world like He told us to. When we're just going to the Lord, saying, "I need this" or "I need that," we're living with just enough for ourselves, but we don't have enough to even get the Gospel out of town, so to speak.

We need to get to the place in our faith that it's not enough until we have too much. I heard a well-known minister say one time that he found out the Lord will hear your prayer at the top of the barrel just as much as at the bottom.

A story in the Old Testament shows us the way God thinks about these things. I think we need to get hold on what God said to David when the prophet Nathan brought a word from God to him. David had committed murder and adultery, and God sent Nathan to confront him about it. Among other things, God said to David, *"And I gave thee thy master's house, and thy master's wives into thy bosom, and gave thee the house of Israel and of Judah; AND IF THAT HAD BEEN TOO LITTLE, I would moreover have given unto thee such and such things"* (2 Sam. 12:8).

God was telling David that if what he had wasn't enough, he needed only to ask, and God would have given him more.

We know from the size of the offering that David gave from his own personal treasury toward the building of the temple, David was a multi-billionaire (1 Chron. 29:3-5). Here God is talking to a multi-billionaire and saying, "If what you had wasn't enough I would have given you more."

We Determine What 'Enough' Is

I'll never forget what the Lord said to my heart one day when I was meditating on this verse. He said, "You see, I let you determine what 'enough' is." Glory to God! I instantly saw what the Lord was saying to me. He will only stop pouring His blessings on us when we stop receiving from Him. I think David was beyond trusting God for his house and chariot payment, don't you? He was certainly beyond what most people would say he *needed*.

Yet, God was meeting him at his level of faith and wasn't asking him if he really needed all that money. That's just the way God is. He has never been One to put a limit on us.

It all comes back to what we can receive. Here is the answer to a question that people have had about the hundredfold return. What difference does it make if God can multiply something a hundredfold, or even a thousandfold for that matter, if you can't receive it?

God can do anything, but how blessed you are isn't based on what God can do, but on what you can receive. Many people have deceived themselves in this area. They claim to be believing God for a hundredfold return when they have never believed Him for a tenfold return yet and gotten it!

The widow woman in the Old Testament discovered that her miracle was according to her faith. Notice the story in Second Kings 4:1-7.

2 KINGS 4:1-7
1 Now there cried a certain woman of the wives of the sons of the prophets unto Elisha, saying, Thy servant my husband is dead; and thou knowest that thy servant did fear the Lord: and the creditor is come to take unto him my two sons to be bondmen.
2 And Elisha said unto her, What shall I do for thee? tell me, what hast thou in the house? And she said, Thine handmaid hath not any thing in the house, save a pot of oil.
3 Then he said, Go, borrow thee vessels abroad of all thy neighbours, even empty vessels: BORROW NOT A FEW.
4 And when thou art come in, thou shalt shut the door upon thee and upon thy sons, and shalt pour out into all those vessels, and thou shalt set aside that which is full.
5 So she went from him, and shut the door upon her and upon her sons, who brought the vessels to her; and she poured out.
6 And it came to pass, when the vessels were full, that she said unto her son, Bring me yet a vessel. And he said unto her, There is not a vessel more. AND THE OIL STAYED.
7 Then she came and told the man of God. And he said, Go, sell the oil, and pay thy debt, and live thou and thy children of the rest.

Did you notice where the miracle stopped? The miracle went as far as her faith went when Elisha told her not to get just a few vessels. The way she measured what God said to her determined how big the miracle was.

If Elisha had told a hundred widows that day to go borrow vessels from their neighbors and not to get just a few, they would each have heard that statement in a different way, because each would have been at a different level of faith for prosperity. Some would have gotten ten, others twenty or thirty or a hundred, but each one of them would have received according to her faith. Some would have thought they were getting a lot when they borrowed thirty vessels, but that doesn't mean that *God* thought thirty was a lot. He left it open-ended so the widow woman could receive as much as she liked. If a thousand barrels wasn't "enough" for her, God would have met her at her level of faith.

God Wants You To Have Too Much!

God's perfect will, as you can see, is for us to receive too much. He said that His blessings would be "*. . . good measure, pressed down, and shaken together, and running over. . .* " (Luke 6:38). If you get a bigger "faith container," you'll be able to catch more of that "running over" part! The truth is, God's blessings are always going to run over what you can receive, but you'll only be able to enjoy what you can receive.

Our problem is that we don't really have a vision of abundance many times because of what things have been like for us in the past. If you aren't careful to guard your mind with the Word of God, your mentality will be formed by the lack that you've experienced up until now.

Peter found that out when the Lord told him to let down his nets (plural) for a catch of fish. He had been fishing all night and had not caught anything, so he wasn't too excited about spending any more time trying. He knew that the fish weren't out there because he had just spent all night trying to find them.

"And Simon answering said unto him, Master, we have toiled all the night, and have taken nothing: nevertheless at thy word I will let down the NET [singular]. *And when they had this done, they inclosed a great multitude of fishes: and their NET* [singular] *brake"* (Luke 5:5,6).

Peter's lack of faith is evident in the fact that he didn't fully obey the Lord. The Lord had said to let down his nets, but he only let down one net. In other words, the Lord had planned on blessing Peter bigger than he had faith to receive. Peter thought that if he had a net full of fish, that would be enough. But what Peter thought was "enough" and what the Lord thought was "enough" were two different things.

Someone said, "Yeah, but I'm happy with where I am financially." Well, is the Lord happy, though? Maybe He wants to do more for you than you even know. Why don't you let Him do it for you?

Chapter 3
Grace To Be Rich

We have seen in Chapter One that Jesus came to redeem us from poverty so that we might be rich.

2 CORINTHIANS 8:9
9 For ye know the grace of our Lord Jesus Christ, that, though he was rich, yet for your sakes he became poor, that ye through his poverty might be rich.

According to this verse, it was the Lord's grace that made us rich. I like to read it this way: "For ye know the *graciousness* of our Lord Jesus Christ. . . . " It sure was gracious of Him to become poor that we might be rich, wasn't it! Thank God, there is grace for our pocketbook.

God's Far-Reaching and All-Encompassing Grace

There are different kinds of grace in the New Testament. Or, we could say that New Testament grace is for more than one area of our lives. We see, for example, that there is *saving* grace (Eph. 2:8); *standing* grace (2 Cor. 12:9); and *serving* grace (Rom. 12:6).

The grace that Second Corinthians 8:9 refers to is saving grace. If you analyze the language this verse uses, you'll see that it is redemptive language. Jesus redeemed us from poverty, and by His grace made us rich. Glory to God! That's good news! I think some people have thought that sounds too good to be true. They'll say, "It can't really mean what it says, can it? That verse must be talking about some sort of *spiritual* riches that Jesus gave us.

No, if you read the context of chapters 8 and 9, you'll find that the entire two chapters are talking about money. I think some Christians have not really gotten a revelation yet that the word "Gospel" means *good news*! But I submit that if something is *not* "too good to be true," then it's probably not really the Gospel.

Jesus told us exactly the same thing the Apostle Paul told us when He said in Luke 4:18 and 19, *"The Spirit of the Lord is upon me, because he hath anointed me TO PREACH THE GOSPEL TO THE POOR; he hath sent me to heal the brokenhearted, to preach deliverance to the captives, and recovering of sight to the blind, to set at liberty them that are bruised, TO PREACH THE ACCEPTABLE YEAR OF THE LORD."*

The Acceptable Year of the Lord

Now, to most of us Westerners, those are terms that don't really register on us as they did on those Jews the day Jesus said that. The reason we miss the meaning of what Jesus said is, we don't know our Old Testament very well. The term "the acceptable year of the Lord" is a reference to the Old Testament year of Jubilee. It is described in detail in Leviticus 25 and Deuteronomy 15. "The acceptable year of the Lord" is also called the year of the Lord's release.

In the year of Jubilee, everyone's debts were canceled

and everyone returned to his possessions that he had lost through debt collection. That's part of our redemption that Jesus came to bring us! He came preaching the Good News to *the poor*!

Most people who claim to preach the Gospel are only preaching about a third of the Gospel. They never mention the other two thirds of what we have been redeemed from. They may be thoroughly born again, but the devil will take advantage of them in other areas of their lives. The Bible tells us that Christ has redeemed us from the curse of the Law (Gal. 3:13), which was threefold. The curse included *poverty*, *sickness*, and *the Second Death* (*see* Deuteronomy 28).

The people who only hear the first part of their redemption will have faith to receive the part that they hear, but they will not have faith for anything else. If they are going to have faith for healing and prosperity, they are going to have to hear the other two thirds of the Gospel, because faith comes by hearing and hearing by the Word of God (Rom. 10:17). Usually, people are told that God wants them poor and sick their whole miserable life until Jesus comes again. So in order for them to believe for prosperity and healing, they are going to have to *unbelieve* some things before they can ever believe the truth. For that reason, people many times have to hear and hear the Word of God in order to displace the lies that have so entangled them spiritually.

Our Redemption Includes Freedom From Poverty

It's interesting that in Luke chapter 4, Jesus mentioned our redemption from poverty first. In most cases, this is the last thing that people hear they have been redeemed from. I believe we have a lot of catching up to do in this area. The church's faith for prosperity is lower than their faith for any other blessing from God.

As I have traveled around the nation preaching the good news of biblical prosperity, I have met more people needing help in this area than any other area. That is because of a lack of teaching on this subject from the Word of God.

In some cases, much of what has been said from the pulpit about money is negative. Therefore, the devil has had a heyday in this area, because he thrives in an atmosphere of unbelief. In order for people to overcome Satan, they have to have Bible knowledge. Faith begins where the will of God is known.

If you don't know that poverty is a curse of the devil (Mal. 3:9; Job 42:10; John 10:10), but were told that it is a blessing from God, then you'll not stand against poverty, because you certainly don't want to resist God, do you! Most of what people have said about money has been unfounded scripturally. You need to have Scripture — chapter and verse — for what people say before you just "swallow" it. And you need not just accept an isolated text somewhere that isn't even in context or in harmony with the rest of the Scriptures or the character of God.

A Loving Father Wants To Meet The Needs of His Children

Jesus revealed God to be a loving Father to us. A father, He said, knows how to give good things to His children, and our heavenly Father God is the same way (Matt. 7:7-11).

"Yes," someone said, "but we really don't know what's good for us." If you have any sense, you do, especially if you have any Bible sense! If you're hungry, you ought to know that it would be good to have something to eat! Psalm 107:9 says, *"For he* [the Lord] *satisfieth the longing soul, and filleth the hungry soul with goodness."* That's pretty simple. Having the things you need is good. If that is true, then having more than you need would be *better*, and having *more than, more than* you need would be *best*!

Throughout the Scriptures, material blessings are called the Lord's goodness.

> **JEREMIAH 33:9**
> **9 And it shall be to me a name of joy, a praise and an honour before all the nations of the earth, which shall hear all the GOOD that I do unto them: and they shall FEAR AND TREMBLE for all the GOODNESS and for all the PROSPERITY that I procure unto it.**

That's a lot of prosperity when people get all shaken up over it!

> **JEREMIAH 31:11,12**
> **11 For the Lord hath redeemed Jacob, and ransomed him from the hand of him that was stronger than he.**
> **12 Therefore they shall come and sing in the height of Zion, and shall flow together to the GOODNESS OF THE LORD, FOR WHEAT, AND FOR WINE, AND FOR OIL, AND FOR THE YOUNG OF THE FLOCK AND OF THE HERD: and their soul shall be as a watered garden; and they shall not sorrow any more at all.**

> **NEHEMIAH 9:25**
> **25 And they took strong cities, and a FAT LAND** [a good land], **and possessed HOUSES FULL OF ALL GOODS,**

wells digged, vineyards, and oliveyards, and fruit trees in ABUNDANCE: so they did eat, and were FILLED, and became FAT, and delighted themselves in thy GREAT GOODNESS.

DEUTERONOMY 28:11,12
11 And the Lord shall make thee plenteous in GOODS, in the fruit of thy body, and in the fruit of thy cattle, and in the fruit of thy ground, in the land which the LORD sware unto thy fathers to give thee.
12 The Lord shall open unto thee his GOOD TREASURE, the heaven to give the rain unto thy land in his season, and to bless all the work of thine hand: and THOU SHALT LEND UNTO MANY NATIONS, AND THOU SHALT NOT BORROW.

People talk about goods and services all week long on the job, but then when they get to church, they call those things "bads"! In other words, they don't want to talk about those things in the "house of God." But anytime you have to change your doctrine to go into the church house, you are either being a hypocrite before you get there, or you're being a hypocrite while you're there.

No, goods are *goods*, not *bads*, and it would take a preacher to get you confused about it.

God's New Testament Goodness

Someone might say, "Yes, but those are just Old Testament verses to the Jews. I don't believe that natural blessings are for us in the New Testament." I would hate to display my ignorance of the New Testament right out in public like that! First of all, the New Testament says that godliness is *profitable unto all things* (that would include financial profit, wouldn't it?), having promise of *the life that now is*, and of the life that is to come" (1 Tim. 4:8). Jesus said that givers can receive a hundredfold *now in this time* (Mark 10:30).

Second, if you are born again, you *are* a Jew.

ROMANS 2:28,29
28 For he is not a Jew, which is one outwardly; neither is that circumcision, which is outward in the flesh:
29 But he is a Jew, which is one INWARDLY; and CIRCUMCISION IS THAT OF THE HEART, in the SPIRIT, and not in the LETTER; whose praise is not of men, but of God.

The promises that God made to Abraham and to his seed in the Old Testament were not to him and his seed after the flesh only, but to us who are the *spiritual* seed of Abraham through faith in Christ (Rom. 4:16; Gal. 3:13,14,29).

Third, Second Corinthians 8:9 just flat said that God's goodness through Jesus has made us rich! His grace is His goodness, isn't it? How good is this grace to make us rich? Second Corinthians 9:8 refers to this same grace of prosperity and says, *"And God is able to make all grace abound toward you; that ye, always having all sufficiency in all things, may abound to every good work."*

I read that verse for years and didn't see how big this blessing really is. Look at that verse in *The Amplified Bible.*

2 CORINTHIANS 9:8 (*Amplified*)
8 And God is able to make all grace (every favor and earthly blessing) come to you in abundance, so that you may always and under all circumstances and whatever the need, be self-sufficient — possessing enough to require no aid or support and furnished in abundance for every good work and charitable donation.

Look at that statement, "possessing enough to require no aid or support." What are you doing when you go down to the bank and take out a loan for a car or a house or when you have to use a credit card to help you buy a set of clothes? You are getting aid from that bank or credit card company. You're not able to buy a particular item with cash, so you're using their money to help you buy that item.

What is this verse telling us — that it's wrong to borrow money? No, it's telling us that God's grace is able to make you richer than that. It's telling us that — if you can receive it — you don't need the bank. In fact, if you take the whole counsel of God on the matter, this verse is telling us that God is able to make *you* the bank!

We Are Above Only, Not Beneath!

God told the Old Testament people that if they would walk in their covenant, they would lend and not have to borrow. He said He would make them the head (financially) and not the tail, that they would be above only (financially) and not beneath. If you're above only, then you're very high financially. If you're the head, you're making all the financial decisions. If you're lending to others, then you're the bank.

Don't you know that the head gets all the blessings and makes all the decisions? Take your dog, for example. When you pet him, you usually pet him on the head. When you feed him a meaty bone, you give the bone to his head. His tail never gets much of anything from you. In fact, your *dog* never gives his tail much of anything! His tail just follows him around wherever he goes. If his head says, "Wag," the tail doesn't have much choice in the matter. The tail has to do whatever your dog tells it to do.

That's what Jesus came to set you free from — living like your dog's tail! You might say, "Brother Jay, what do you mean by that?" Well, every time the credit card company says, "Pay," you say, "Okay, I guess I don't have any choice in the matter." Jesus came to set you free from being a slave to the lender. How free? It's according to your faith.

You Must *Receive* the Grace of God

You may say, "Well, I just don't know how I could ever buy a car or a house with cash." This verse is telling you how. It's by His grace. But if you can't receive what the Bible has to say about the matter, then there may not be a way.

Most people have allowed our society to form their beliefs and their mentality, rather than letting the Bible mold their thinking. You have to divorce yourself from everyone else's ways of thinking and believing if you're going to get different results than everyone else gets. You have to go against the grain, so to speak. You can't just float through life and allow the current to take you where it wants you to go. The current of unbelief in the world is strong and will take you where everyone else is going, and that is down the tube! You're going to have to get out your paddle of faith and start going against the flow.

"Yes, but I just don't have that kind of money." I didn't say you did. I said you have that kind of *grace*. If you can receive the grace (and this book is written to show you how), then His grace and your faith will cause the money to come.

"But I'm just a single mom," someone else will say. Grace is for everyone. It's for widows, retired folks, children, people in third-world countries, orphans, welfare recipients, and whosoever will believe. It's not a matter of who you are; it's a matter of your faith and His grace.

Am I implying that everyone can be rich? No, the Bible is flat *saying* it!

"Well I don't know about that, Brother Jay. My aunt Susie was a good person and served God all her life, but she never got rich." I'm sure Aunt Susie was a good person, but you don't get prosperity by how good you are; you get prosperity because of how good *He* is, and you get it by faith, not by serving God for a long time. Certainly, we are to serve God, but our serving Him is to be a response to His love for us, not in order to earn His blessings.

Grace is a free gift. It's not something you can earn by anything you may or may not do. If you think about it, grace is for the worst of people as much as it is for the best of people.

Let's take this one step further. If you study the subject of grace closely, you'll find that there is more to the grace of God than just undeserved generosity. Grace involves the power of God resting on you to give you supernatural ability.

Notice the following verses.

EPHESIANS 3:7
7 Whereof I [Paul] **was made a minister, according to the GIFT OF THE GRACE OF GOD given unto me by the EFFECTUAL WORKING OF HIS POWER.**

GALATIANS 2:8,9
8 For he that WROUGHT EFFECTUALLY IN PETER to the apostleship of the circumcision, the same was MIGHTY IN ME toward the Gentiles:
9 And when James, Cephas, and John, who seemed to be pillars, perceived the GRACE THAT WAS GIVEN UNTO ME, they gave to me and Barnabas the right hands of fellowship; that we should go unto the heathen, and they unto the circumcision.

1 PETER 4:10,11
10 As every man hath received the gift, even so minister the same one to another, as good stewards of the MANIFOLD GRACE OF GOD.
11 If any man speak, let him speak as the oracles of God; if any man minister, let him do it as of the ABILITY WHICH GOD GIVETH: that God in all things may be glorified through Jesus Christ, to whom be praise and dominion for ever and ever. Amen.

According to these scriptures, grace is the effectual working of His power. Grace is the ability of God upon you to enable you to go beyond your own ability. Of course, these verses are speaking of serving grace, but no matter which area of our lives His grace may be applied, it is always the same thing: Grace is His being free and generous toward us with His power in order to take us further than we could ever go by ourselves!

As we have seen from Second Corinthians chapters 8 and 9, there is grace to prosper us financially. Notice 2 Corinthians 8:1-4.

2 CORINTHIANS 8:1-4
1 Moreover, brethren, we do you to wit [or, we want you to know] **of the GRACE OF GOD bestowed on the churches of Macedonia;**
2 How that in a great trial of affliction the abundance of their joy and their deep poverty abounded

unto the riches of their liberality.
3 For to their power, I bear record, yea, and BEYOND THEIR POWER they were willing of themselves;
4 Praying us with much intreaty that we would receive the gift, and take upon us the fellowship of the ministering to the saints.

Paul wanted the Corinthians to know of a move of God among the churches of Macedonia in the area of prosperity. He said that the grace of God on them was taking them *beyond* their own ability financially. The Greek literally says that God's grace was taking them "exceedingly above and beyond" their own financial ability. I like that "exceeding" part, don't you? God's power is available to take you further than you ever dreamed you could go!

This subject has been a tremendous blessing to me ever since I began to understand it. Second Corinthians is telling us that God is willing to invest His power into helping us prosper financially. What a thought! That means there is what we could call a "prosperity anointing."

Notice again now what Jesus said He came to preach.

LUKE 4:18,19
18 The Spirit of the Lord is upon me, because he hath anointed me to PREACH THE GOSPEL TO THE POOR....
19 To preach THE ACCEPTABLE YEAR OF THE LORD.

If you study the message that Jesus preached, His message was the anointing. He was anointed to preach His message, but His message was the anointing. In other words, that was what He came to tell the poor man. He was preaching that the anointing on Him was able to break the yoke of, among other things, *poverty*!

Jesus Came To Empower Us For Prosperity

How do we know for sure that was His message? Acts 10:36-38 tells us.

ACTS 10:36-38
36 The word which God sent unto the children of Israel, preaching peace by Jesus Christ: (he is Lord of all:)
37 That WORD [or message], I say, ye know, WHICH WAS PUBLISHED THROUGHOUT ALL JUDAEA, and began from Galilee, after the baptism which John preached [that's when the anointing came on Him];
38 How God ANOINTED Jesus of Nazareth WITH THE HOLY GHOST AND WITH POWER: who went about doing good, and healing all that were oppressed of the devil; for God was with him.

In other words, Jesus preached the anointing everywhere He went. He preached it, but He also *demonstrated* the anointing. *Demonstration* preaches something just as good as *talking about it* does.

New Testament Demonstrations

We can see Jesus throughout His entire ministry ministering to people's financial and material needs under that anointing. Just to name a few cases, He turned water into wine (John 2:1-11), multiplied bread for four- and five thousand men, plus women and children (Matt. 14:21; Mark 6:44; Luke 9:14; John 6:10), He helped Peter and his partners catch more fish than they could handle (Luke 5:4-7), and, on one occasion, He supernaturally paid His and Peter's taxes (Matt. 17:27).

'Blessing' Defined

Now think about Deuteronomy 8:18: *"But thou shalt remember the Lord thy God: for it is he that GIVETH THEE POWER TO GET WEALTH, that he may establish his covenant which he sware unto thy fathers, as it is this day."*

Here again is proof that God is willing to invest His power in our prosperity. That verse certainly wouldn't be referring to any other power than Holy Ghost power, would it? It has to be God's power, because Deuteronomy 8:18 says that it comes from Him. The Bible says that power is the anointing that removes burdens and destroys yokes (Isa. 10:27). Anyone who says poverty isn't a yoke or a burden has never been poor. From the beginning, God has used His power to cause covenant men to prosper financially, even in the worst of situations.

This verse in Deuteronomy 8 says that God sware or promised this power to the children of Israel's fathers, which would be Abraham, Isaac, and Jacob. In looking through the Book of Genesis, I could find no reference to God giving these men an oath of power to get wealth. The nearest statement I could find to this affect was, "I will bless thee" (Gen. 12:2). As I studied it further, I noticed that every time God said, "I will bless thee," there was a financial increase connected to that blessing. It happened for Abraham, Isaac, and Jacob without fail.

When I studied the word "blessing," I found that the word meant *an empowering to succeed or prosper*. Just as a curse conveys with it the power of Satan, a blessing carries with it the power of God.

Isn't it amazing that Christians believe that a witch doctor overseas can put curses on people and cause their crops to be destroyed or their flocks to die, but those same Christians won't tell those people that God has any power to cause them to get rich!

"Well, we don't want to preach that prosperity gospel over there," they say. "Those people are poor. This is just an American Gospel." But grace isn't just for Americans! You'd *better* preach the prosperity message to them, or they'll be poor the next time you see them too.

That's a silly attitude to take toward preaching the full Gospel to the poor. That would be like telling someone who preaches salvation to cannibals way back in the bush, "You can't preach that message over there; these people aren't *saved*. Why, if you preach that to them, they'll *eat* you."

No, if you *don't* preach the Gospel to them, they'll eat you!

You have to preach the gospel of salvation to sinners if you want the power of God to come into their lives to change that devilish nature that's in them. The same is true about the power of God to prosper them. If you don't preach the Word to them, that power won't work, because the power works by faith, and faith comes by hearing (Rom. 10:17).

We need to preach this message in order for this prosperity anointing to work fully. Look at what that anointing did for Abraham. The Bible says that right after God blessed him, he was very rich in cattle, in silver, and in gold (Gen. 13:2). Abraham's servant said, "*. . . the Lord hath BLESSED my master greatly; and he is become great: and he hath given him flocks, and herds, and silver, and* *gold, and menservants, and maidservants, and camels, and asses"* (Gen. 24:35).

Abraham got so blessed that he and Lot couldn't even live in the same regions of the country. Their flocks and herds were too big to fit in the same place (Gen. 13:6)!

The same blessing came on Isaac, and he reaped a hundredfold harvest right in the middle of a famine.

GENESIS 26:1,2,6,12-16
1 And there was a famine in the land, beside the first famine that was in the days of Abraham. And Isaac went unto Abimelech king of the Philistines unto Gerar.
2 And the Lord appeared unto him, and said, Go not down into Egypt; dwell in the land which I shall tell thee of....
6 And Isaac dwelt in Gerar....
12 Then Isaac sowed in that land, and received in the same year an hundredfold: and the Lord BLESSED him.
13 And the man waxed great, and went forward, and grew until he became very great:
14 For he had possession of flocks, and possession of herds, and great store of servants: and the Philistines envied him.
15 For all the wells which his father's servants had digged in the days of Abraham his father, the Philistines had stopped them, and filled them with earth.
16 And Abimelech said unto Isaac, Go from us; for thou art much mightier than we.

That blessing was certainly more than a nice religious cliché. The blessing obviously involved the power of God to prosper everything Isaac touched. Now notice what happened when this blessing came on Jacob. You remember Jacob worked for his uncle Laban, but Laban kept changing his terms of pay. Well, Jacob finally got tired of the whole ordeal and put in his resignation.

> **GENESIS 30:27,28**
> **27 And Laban said unto him, I pray thee, if I have found favour in thine eyes, tarry: for I have learned by experience that THE LORD HATH BLESSED ME FOR THY SAKE.**
> **28 And he said, Appoint me thy wages, and I will give it.**

I like that! Here is an employer chasing a blessed man of God down and offering him any wages he asks for, as long as he works for him instead of the competition. Glory to God! Did you notice that God was putting His power on the whole company just to get the blessing to His covenant man, Jacob? The Lord will do the same thing for you.

Laban told Jacob that the little flock that was there when he arrived had become a great multitude because of the Lord's blessing. Finally, Jacob decided that he would stay and work for Laban, but only if he gave him all the spotted and speckled animals. Laban was delighted, so what Jacob had asked was done. Laban probably reasoned, "I still have more than when Jacob came to town, so I'm really no worse off."

> **GENESIS 30:43**
> **43 And the man [Jacob] increased exceedingly, and had much cattle, and maidservants, and menservants, and camels, and asses.**

Later, Jacob said to Rachel and Leah, his wives, "*Thus God hath taken away the cattle of your father, and given them to me*" (Gen. 31:9). The blessing worked for Jacob right in the middle of the worst of circumstances.

God Will Bless Your Employer To Get a Blessing to You

Somcone said, "Well, you don't know how mean my boss is."

Jacob didn't have such a hot boss himself, did he? Yet he prospered right in the middle of that mess. God will do what He has to do to get blessings to you if you'll talk right and stay in faith.

This same blessing is for us today. What is a blessing? It is an empowerment from God to prosper.

Galatians 3:13 and 14 will have more meaning to you now that you know what a blessing is.

> **GALATIANS 3:13,14**
> **13 Christ hath REDEEMED US FROM THE CURSE OF THE LAW, being made a curse for us: for it is written, Cursed is every one that hangeth on a tree:**
> **14 That the BLESSING OF ABRAHAM might come on the Gentiles through Jesus Christ; that we might receive THE PROMISE OF THE SPIRIT through faith.**

Thank God, Jesus didn't leave us to fend for ourselves in this area. Our redemption covers this area of our lives as well as every other. I believe that as we learn what to do to receive this grace of prosperity, we as the Body of Christ will see a tremendous move of the power of God in the area of financial miracles.

Every other area of redemption that the Church lost sight of in the Dark Ages has been restored to her over the last few hundred years. When Martin Luther stood up and said, "Salvation is by grace, not by works," the Church began to have restoration of everything we lost. First, we saw holiness restored. Then we saw the baptism of the Holy Ghost, the gifts of the Spirit, and healing restored. Later, living by faith in the Word was restored in the Charismatic and teaching revivals. We're now in a time when the Church's money is being restored to her.

Let's believe God for that restoration. Let's learn how to flow with this anointing that causes money to come to us.

Chapter 4
Prospering God's Way

When we talk about prosperity, we're not talking about what the world does to prosper. We're talking about prospering in line with the Word and according to its principles.

Unfortunately, most believers have only been familiar with the world's kind of prosperity. All their lives, they've seen people lie, cheat, and steal their way to wealth, so much so that people have the idea that money itself is evil. They have never had the Word of God taught to them along this line. Most preachers are afraid to talk about money, and that's exactly the way the devil wants it.

Real Prosperity Is Without Sorrow

For this reason, the only thing most Christians know is what they've seen in the world. The world's way of prospering is the only way they believe they can prosper. Prosperity that comes any other way than through God and His Word will always have a lot of sorrow with it, and that's really not prosperity at all. I'm talking about what the Bible says in Proverbs 10:22.

PROVERBS 10:22
22 The blessing of the Lord, it maketh rich, and HE ADDETH NO SORROW WITH IT.

Prosperity that comes through our relationship to God and obedience to His will adds no sorrow with it. That's the real prosperity. Prosperity is about much more than money. God wants our entire life to prosper, spirit, soul, and body — in our marriage, home, family, and every area of our life.

There are many people who have money who would give it all away just to be set free from torment in some area of their lives or to be healed of a terminal disease. Real prosperity comes through having Jesus in your life and through His Word setting you free. Many who prosper in the world do so only to use their money to live more miserably and die younger because of rampant sin and abuse of some kind.

The Bible tells us that there are two ways to prosper: The *world's* way and *God's* way.

PSALM 73:3,12
3 For I was envious at the foolish, when I saw THE PROSPERITY OF THE WICKED....
12 Behold, these are the ungodly, who PROSPER IN THE WORLD; they increase in riches.

PSALM 37:7
7 Rest in the Lord, and wait patiently for him: fret not thyself because of him WHO PROSPERETH IN HIS WAY, because of the man who bringeth wicked devices to pass.

PROVERBS 10:2,3
2 TREASURES OF WICKEDNESS profit nothing: but righteousness delivereth from death.

3 The Lord will not suffer the soul of the righteous to famish: but he casteth away the substance of the wicked.

All of these verses show us people who prospered apart from God. They had gone about gathering wealth their own way without the blessing of God. Notice what happens to wealth gotten the wrong way.

PROVERBS 15:6,16
6 In the house of the righteous is much treasure: but IN THE REVENUES OF THE WICKED IS TROUBLE....
16 Better is little with the fear of the Lord THAN GREAT TREASURE AND TROUBLE THEREWITH.

Verse 16 didn't say that it's better to have a little than to have a lot. It said that it's better to have God in what you do have than not to serve God and have all the money you could ever want with the curse in it. If you walk with God, He'll bless what you have and give you a whole lot more without all the trouble. I'll tell you right now, you don't want a bunch of money without God in your life. Many rich people without God are popping pills to get to sleep at night, worrying about someone "taking it all away from them."

Many people who have obtained money in the world apart from God didn't get what they were looking for when they set out to make those millions. They thought, *If I could just make a million dollars, I wouldn't have anymore problems.* The fact is, they have more problems now than they had when they were broke. Now they've got doctor bills because of their ulcers, and they've got lawyer fees coming out their ears, so to speak, because they have to watch their back constantly lest someone take advantage of them. Their wife is wanting a divorce because the husband is never home, and the kids are running the streets getting into trouble. They have been deceived by money (Mark 4:19).

That's "run of the mill" for a vast number of folks in the world. Christians have seen that and thought, *If that's the only way to obtain wealth, then forget prosperity!*

Base Your Doctrine on the *Word*, Not the *World*

It's not the only way to obtain wealth! That has been the problem with the Church. We've based our doctrine on what we've seen in the world rather than on the Word of God.

Just because you may not know anyone who served God and became wealthy doesn't mean that prosperity is not available. The Word says that it is available. We can't base our doctrine on what we see happening to ungodly men. And we can't get our doctrine from the news media or from some poll that someone conducted. Those polls don't factor in the fact that 80 percent of the people surveyed are dead spiritually, and about 99.9 percent of them aren't going about prospering God's way.

Surveys tell us that only about three percent of the world's population ever really obtains wealth. If those figures are true, then why follow what the world is doing to obtain prosperity. That sounds like a 97 percent failure rate to me! Why not find out what God's Word says about prosperity and act on that. It is 100-percent guaranteed to work because Jesus personally guarantees the Word of God Himself (Heb. 7:22).

God has the answer in His Word to every question you'll ever have in life, and He has the answers in this area of prosperity as well. The first thing you must do is to resolve that whatever you see in the Word of God, you're going to walk in the light of it, no matter what you think about what it is you are seeing.

The Word must be final authority in your life, case closed. When you find what the Word says, that Word rules every decision, and it's not up for debate. You'll not hold any conference meetings with your mind and your flesh about what the Word says, because you're not operating out of your mind or your flesh's whims, but out of your spirit. Even if your flesh is in turmoil, your friends laugh at you, and your soul is pouting, there is no debate and there is no retreat. You're acting on the Word of God. That's when you are ready for loads of prosperity without all the sorrow of the world in it.

The reason I covered all that before we look at God's way of prospering is, it takes a resolve in faith in order to walk this thing out. Don't you know that if prospering were easy, everyone would be prospering? Don't you know that if people really prepared themselves ahead of time, they wouldn't be quitting and saying, "That faith stuff doesn't work?" Faith *does* work; it's just that they thought faith was a get-rich-quick scheme of some kind that was going to make them millionaires overnight. No, the devil will resist you, and you need to know that ahead of time.

Now let's look at God's way of prospering us. First, we must understand that God's ways don't really make sense to the natural mind. To the natural or carnal man, they just don't seem right.

ISAIAH 55:8,9
8 For my thoughts are not your thoughts, neither are your ways my ways, saith the Lord.
9 For as the heavens are higher than the earth, so are my ways higher than your ways, and my thoughts than your thoughts.

PROVERBS 14:12
12 THERE IS A WAY WHICH SEEMETH RIGHT UNTO A MAN, but the end thereof are the ways of death.

The reason God's ways are higher than the natural man's ways is, they require that you walk by faith. If your method of acquiring wealth doesn't require faith in God's Word, it'll be wrong every time.

Divine prosperity comes from the Word of God.

PSALM 1:1-6
1 Blessed [empowered to prosper] **is the man that walketh not IN THE COUNSEL OF THE UNGODLY, nor standeth in the way of sinners, nor sitteth in the seat of the scornful.**
2 But his DELIGHT is in THE LAW OF THE LORD; and IN HIS LAW doth he MEDITATE DAY AND NIGHT.
3 And he shall be like a tree planted by the rivers of water, that bringeth forth his fruit in his season; his leaf also shall not wither; and WHATSOEVER HE DOETH SHALL PROSPER.

4 The ungodly are not so: but are like the chaff which the wind driveth away.
5 Therefore the ungodly shall not stand in the judgment, nor sinners in the congregation of the righteous.
6 For the Lord knoweth THE WAY OF THE RIGHTEOUS: but the WAY OF THE UNGODLY shall perish.

This passage once again compares the way of the world with the way of God. God's Word is His constitution. God's Word is His *modus operandi.* Every kingdom or government has a constitution by which it operates. The word "constitution" means *the way in which a government, state, or society is organized*; *a system of fundamental laws and principles*; *a decree or regulation*; *a document or set of documents in which these laws and principles are written down*; or *the makeup, structure, or arrangement of a government.*

We Are Free From Sin, Satan, and the World

There are two spiritual kingdoms operating on the earth, and both operate on spiritual laws. They are the kingdom of Satan and the Kingdom of God (Col. 1:13). Each of these kingdoms has a system of operating in order to bring about its intentions. Satan is the lord of death and intends to rule with the law of sin and death — the curse — over all who will let him. Jesus is the Lord of life and intends to rule in your life with His blessing.

Thank God, the law of the Spirit of life in Christ Jesus has made us free from the law of sin and death (Rom. 8:2). We as believers have been translated out of the kingdom of darkness into the Kingdom of God.

However, in order to enjoy the full potential of His blessings, we must renew our minds to His constitution. Most Christians have learned all they know about prosperity from the world. Don't you know that system has trained you to stay poor?

The only reason a Christian would live out his life here on the earth and not become prosperous would be because he didn't walk in God's way of prospering. His ways were unconstitutional. Don't misunderstand me, it's easy to do. All you have to do in order to be unconstitutional is *nothing*. But if you want God to direct your path financially, you're going to have to acknowledge Him in all your ways, including your financial ways (Prov. 3:6). You're going to have to acknowledge His Word on the subject, and you're going to have to acknowledge His Kingdom work with your giving.

We must constantly check with the Word to see if what we are doing financially is right. Is what we are doing authorized by, subject to, and dependent upon the constitution — God's Word? If so, the blessing is on it automatically. You don't have to pray that the Lord will bless you, because spiritual laws are already blessed. If you'll operate in them, you'll make your own way prosperous, and you'll have good success (Joshua 1:8). If you do the right things with your money, you won't have to pray, "Lord, bless me." All you have to do to enjoy Kingdom blessings is to walk in the light of Kingdom principles and talk right.

So many times, people's problems are not something they did just one time. Most of the time, it's a matter of their mode of operation. We've all heard people say things such as, "My rule of thumb is just try to work real hard and save. . . " and so forth.

It Takes More Than Hard Work To Walk In God's Prosperity

Don't misunderstand me. We need to work and be wise with our money, but a lot of people who have a good work ethic don't make much money when you compare it to the blessing of Abraham. Some of the hardest-working people in the world are the poorest people in the world. It takes more than good hard work in order to walk in divine prosperity.

PSALM 127:1
1 Except the Lord build the house, they labour in vain that build it: except the Lord keep the city, the watchman waketh but in vain.

You can work real hard under a curse and lose everything you've ever worked for. Unless you get "the blessing of the Lord that maketh rich" in your finances, the curse that is in the earth will eat your lunch, so to speak. I think Ecclesiastes 10:10 describes very well what happens to most people.

ECCLESIASTES 10:10
10 If the iron be blunt [or, if the ax is dull]**, and he do not whet the edge, then must he put to more strength: but wisdom is profitable to direct.**

An ax is a tool used to harvest trees. This verse is describing a person who works very hard at harvesting trees, but never takes the time to sharpen his ax. The result is that he knocks himself out working real hard, but gets very little done compared to what he could have gotten done if he had used more wisdom.

Many Christians are the same way when it comes to harvesting finances. They knock themselves out working real hard, but have never taken the time to sharpen their ax. Your faith is your ax. You would be wise to take the time to sit down with your Bible and sharpen your faith with the Word. Then when you swing, the bark will start flying!

Spending Time With the Word Is Invaluable

The Lord will also give you invaluable direction during your time with Him in His Word that will save you precious time and money. He may tell you that you're not even in the right woods! You may have run out into the first woods you saw and started chopping, because you didn't think you had the time to seek the Lord on the matter. I can tell you from experience that it will take you a lot longer to get ahead financially if you don't seek Him than it will if you take time to hear from Heaven and get in the right woods (*see* Second Chronicles 26:5).

It's not enough just to work real hard. Someone

might say, "Brother Jay, are you telling us just to be lazy and not work?" No, I'm telling you not to be lazy spiritually. You can be a workaholic and be lazy spiritually.

> **HEBREWS 6:12**
> **12 That ye be not slothful, but followers of them who THROUGH FAITH AND PATIENCE INHERIT THE PROMISES.**

Unless you are doing the things that the Bible says to do to activate your faith financially, the law of sin and death (the curse) that is in the earth will erode away at every advancement you make. You'll get a $500 bonus, and the refrigerator will go out. You'll take a step forward and fall two steps behind. It takes faith to counteract the current of the curse that is in the earth. The Bible says, "*. . . This is the victory that overcometh* [supersedes; prevails over] *the world, even our faith*" (1 John 5:4).

Faith Will Cause You To Rise Above the World System

The Greek word translated "world" in this verse is "kosmos." It means *arrangement*. The root word from which the word "kosmos" comes is "komizo" and means *to provide*; *to take care of*; *to carry off from harm*. In other words, this verse is saying, "This is the victory that supersedes and prevails over the way the world's system (over which Satan is god) has arranged to provide for you, *even your faith*!" The world system has made arrangements to take care of you, but, blessed be

God, God has set up a system of taking care of you financially as well, and this system is all tapped in to by your faith in His Word!

In other words, faith is the key to unlocking all the fundamental principles and spiritual laws in the Word of God.

Giving 'Hard' Is As Important As Working Hard

Most people need more of a faith ethic and less of a work ethic. They need to get a rule of thumb, such as, "Give, and it shall be given unto you" (Luke 6:38), "Bring ye all the tithes into the storehouse, and I'll pour you out a blessing that there shall not be room enough to receive" (Mal. 3:10), and "Seek ye first the kingdom of God (with your money), and all these things shall be added unto you" (Matt. 6:33). If the Word was their rule of thumb, that's what would be coming out of them, and that's what would be happening for them — the Word!

Someone said, "What do you mean by that?" The Word says, "Give, and it shall be given unto you." (Luke 6:38). When was the last time someone handed you a five-hundred or one-thousand dollar check? If your answer is, "No one ever has," then ask yourself the question according to the Word (which is your constitution — it answers all your questions), "Why not?" The only reason that wouldn't be happening to you according to the Word is, you haven't done it for anyone else.

Someone might say, "Well, I know that works for you, Brother Jay, but I'm not a preacher like you are. I know people do that for preachers sometimes." But there you go again. You've gotten away from the Word. Luke 6:38 didn't say this works for *preachers*; it says giving works for *givers*. If we as believers would fight for the Word as hard as we fight against it sometimes, we'd be further along than most of us are.

Look what God said to the children of Israel in Psalm 81:13 and 16.

> **PSALM 81:13,16**
> **13 Oh that my people had hearkened unto me, and Israel had WALKED IN MY WAYS. . . .**
> **16 He should have fed them also with THE FINEST OF WHEAT: AND WITH HONEY OUT OF THE ROCK should I have satisfied thee.**

God was telling these people what their life could have been like if they had walked in His ways of prosperity. Many Christians live out their entire life wandering in the land of "get by" and "make do," but never getting into the land of "the finest that there is." The reason once again is, according to the constitution, they didn't walk in God's way of prospering them.

God's Prosperity Was Designed for *You*!

You can wander around your whole life in the wilderness and your shoes not wear out if you want, but God has something better for you. He has the finest of cars and houses and clothes. Prosperity is not meant for someone else! God meant it for you! Just because some ungodly people have nice things doesn't mean their things are inherently evil. If you get the same kinds of things, they'll be holy!

Money has no inherent nature of its own. It takes on the nature of the person who possesses it. We know that's true, because God caused wise men (Persian astrologers) to bring money to Mary and Joseph to finance their flight into Egypt with Jesus. No doubt those wise men got that money by fortune-telling. To most Christians, that was evil money. But God cleaned that money up and used it for His own benefit!

God said in Isaiah 48:17, *"Thus saith the Lord, thy Redeemer, the Holy One of Israel; I am the Lord thy God WHICH TEACHETH THEE TO PROFIT, WHICH LEADETH THEE BY THE WAY THAT THOU SHOULDEST GO."*

God doesn't want just to hand you something every time you have a need, He wants you to grow up and learn to operate in the laws that govern prosperity so that you have a continuous flow of abundance in your life and can be used by Him to bless others.

It's not enough to know that God wants to prosper us. We must know the way He does it. That is the main thing that Israel missed (Heb. 3:10). Moses drew close to God and got to know His *ways.* But Israel only got to know what God *did* (Ps. 103:7).

We need to let God teach us His ways of profiting. He's been around a lot longer that we have and is much wiser than we are. If we will listen to what He has to say in His Word, we can begin to take on His wisdom and walk in His ways. That, after all, is what the Word was given to us for. His Word will do the same thing for us that it does for Him.

God wants us to live in abundance, not bounce from financial miracle to financial miracle, so to speak. We were never supposed to live by gifts of the Spirit (1 Cor. 12:7-11), which manifest as the Spirit wills, but by every word that proceeds from the mouth of God (Deut. 8:3). The Word of God is for everyday living. Besides, don't you want to be one who God can speak to in order to bless someone else with a financial miracle? If you do, keep reading and learn how!

Chapter 5
Heavenly Banking

A couple of years ago, a pastor told me about something that happened in his church, and I have never forgotten it. In the process of their church growing, they outgrew their church building and needed to purchase one which would give them space to continue to grow. The building that the Lord led them to cost approximately $500,000. At the time, they only had 125 people attending on Sunday mornings, and the bank wasn't willing to loan them the entire amount of money needed to move into the building.

The bank finally agreed to loan them $325,000 on the building if the church could come up with $175,000 in cash to make up the difference. As the pastor sought God on the matter, he knew in his heart that the people wouldn't give that amount of money into a building-fund program within the time frame they'd been given to raise the money. Yet this pastor sensed in his heart that he needed to set up a bond program and make bonds available to his congregation. Any bonds that weren't sold to the congregation, he knew he could make available to some investors who were interested.

When he presented the program to the congregation, within two weeks, they purchased the entire $175,000 in bonds. The pastor knew that the Lord had led him, but he was absolutely shocked at the amount of money that his people had lying around and at the speed at which they bought the bonds.

When this pastor told me that story, I thought to myself, *That's exactly where the Body of Christ is today. They can trust a man's contract and signature that says, "I'll pay back all of your money plus interest," but they can't trust the Word of God when He says He will return all the money many-fold that they* give *into His work.*

The Body of Christ has used the world's methods of investing and have gotten the return everyone else in the world has gotten. There is certainly not anything wrong with putting your money into an earthly investment in order to get a return, but there *is* something wrong with not being able to believe God's Word when He said He would bless your *giving* in a much bigger way.

Heavenly Investing

There may be times that the Lord will lead you to invest money in an earthly investment, especially if that's the level you can believe God on. But there is a level of faith that will bring you a much greater return than anything man has ever given you. It's called the law of sowing and reaping.

You need to seek the Lord on the use of natural investments and allow Him to lead you. But one thing is certain, if you never "feel led" to *give* money into the work of God, then you're really not being led. He'll always lead you to put your money into things that will bring you the best return, and there is no better return on your money than what you'll get from what you've given to God. The Spirit of God will always lead you in line with the Word of God, and the Word is very clear on the subject of giving. Don't be a fool over money — you could lose it all!

LUKE 12:15-21
15 And he [Jesus] said unto them, Take heed, and beware of covetousness: for a man's life consisteth not in the abundance of the things which he possesseth.
16 And he spake a parable unto them, saying, The ground of a certain rich man brought forth plentifully:
17 And he thought within himself, saying, What shall I do, because I have no room where to bestow my fruits?
18 And he said, This will I do: I will pull down my barns, and build greater; and there will I bestow all my fruits and my goods.
19 And I will say to my soul, Soul, thou hast much goods laid up for many years; take thine ease, eat, drink, and be merry.
20 But God said unto him, THOU FOOL, this night thy soul shall be required of thee: then whose shall those things be, which thou hast provided?
21 So is he that layeth up treasure for himself, and is not rich toward God.

It's important to note from this passage that it wasn't that there was something wrong with this man having more blessings than he had room to contain. God, in fact, said that He would pour us out a blessing we wouldn't have room enough to receive (Mal. 3:10). So it wasn't wrong for the man to be rich. It was wrong that he wasn't rich *toward God*. That simply means he didn't give any of his abundance to God. He was putting his faith in the money he had laid up on the earth, rather than God, to take care of him.

How do you keep your faith in God active? *Through your giving!*

It Pays To Be Rich Toward God

There is no nation or economy on the planet that can guarantee you a better return on your money than the Kingdom of God can. I'm sure those people in that church I told you about were glad for an opportunity to invest their money in something that was going to give them a return, but they probably have no idea what they missed by not *giving* that money to the church and believing God to multiply and return it back to them.

In our society, folks get excited if they get a 20-percent return on an investment. God doesn't even talk percentages of return in His Word. He talks about giving you a return that is multiplied many-fold. Just think about it: *One*fold is a one-hundred-percent return! In other words if you received a onefold return from the Lord, that means He doubled your money and gave it back to you!

But you can't find anywhere in the Word that God mentions a onefold return. He starts up around thirtyfold (Matt. 13:8,23; Mark 4:8,20). Why has the Church been doing what the world is doing when we have an opportunity like that to invest? I'll tell you why: *unbelief.*

We find in the Word that God mentions this banking system over and over again. It is Heaven's banking system, and it is based on Heaven's economy. Heaven's economy is the only economy that can afford this kind of return.

You as a believer have a heavenly bank account just as you have a natural bank account. Your heavenly account works in much the same way your natural one does, only your heavenly account is governed by *God's* way of doing things, not man's. His ways are higher than man's ways (Isa. 55:9), and His returns are higher than any man can give also.

In order to operate in this banking system, it will require faith in the Word of God. All God's banking regulations are found there, and He cannot violate them, because

He can't lie. If a banker down here in our economy ever violated one of our nation's banking regulations, we could hold him to the regulation in court and get the money that belongs to us. Well, God said in His Word that He would give you a return on all the money that you invest into His kingdom, and He wants you to hold Him to that.

The Sovereignty of God

Someone might say, "Brother Jay, I wouldn't talk like that if I were you. God is a sovereign God, and we can't make Him do something that He may not want to do." Well, God isn't like you are. You may say something and not really mean it or want to do what you said, but God doesn't. You may make a promise and break it, but God can't. He can't afford to. His Word is the only thing that holds all of Heaven and earth together.

God's Word is simply a revelation of what God is eager to do for you. His will isn't passive, as ours is at times. His will is His resolve, and it is full of determination.

You may promise your children to take them where they want to go for vacation this year if they get a straight-A report card, and then hope they get one B, so you don't have to keep your word. But God isn't like that. Yes, God is a sovereign God, but most people who say that really don't know what that means. The word "sovereign" means *supreme in authority*, *chief,* or *highest*.

Certainly, God is the Most High God. There is no one who can rule over Him. He is under no external restraints or limits, but He has limited *Himself* with His own Word. There are things that He can't do, because He *said* that He can't. There are also things that He *must* do if you hold Him to His Word, because He said He would do them.

People have the idea that God's sovereignty enables Him to do whatever He wants to do, whenever He wants to do it, for whoever He wants to do it. But that is only partly true. God had the ability to do whatever He wanted to do, so He said, "I'll do whatever I *said* I would do."

Did you get that! In other words, since God is sovereign and can do whatever He wants to do, He, by His sovereignty, made His Word sovereign.

PSALM 138:2
2 I will worship toward thy holy temple, and praise thy name for thy lovingkindness and for thy truth: for THOU HAST MAGNIFIED THY WORD ABOVE ALL THY NAME.

The Bible in the *Basic English* translation says, "For You have made Your Word greater than all Your Name." God is governed by His own Word. He invited us to hold Him to His Word so that He can bless us (Isa. 43:25,26). He said that if you sow seed into the Kingdom of God, you'll get a return from your seed. Those are some of His banking regulations. Act on them in faith and then take His Word to Him in prayer, and the Word will work for you.

Magnify the Provision, Not the Problem

Don't go on and on in prayer about the problem — go on and on in prayer about the *provisions* that have been made in His Word. Magnify His Word as He does, and you'll be in agreement with Him.

Let's notice some scriptures that mention this "heavenly banking system."

PHILIPPIANS 4:15-17
15 Now ye Philippians know also, that in the beginning of the gospel, when I departed from Macedonia, no church communicated with me as concerning giving and receiving, but ye only.
16 For even in Thessalonica ye sent once and again unto my necessity.
17 Not because I desire a gift: but I desire fruit that may abound TO YOUR ACCOUNT.

MATTHEW 6:19,20
19 Lay not up for yourselves treasures upon earth, where moth and rust doth corrupt, and where thieves break through and steal:
20 But lay up for yourselves TREASURES IN HEAVEN, where neither moth nor rust doth corrupt, and where thieves do not break through nor steal.

Someone might say, "Yes, Brother Jay, but those verses are talking just about things that we give to God because He needs them, and when we get to Heaven, we'll get our reward."

But to say that is to add to what these verses said. First of all, Jesus didn't say that you need to give because God needs the money, He said to give because *you* need the money! Didn't He say to lay up *for yourselves* treasures in Heaven? Doesn't that mean what is says? Did Jesus say what He meant, or should we change that verse and correct it for Him?

No, Jesus said what He meant, and He meant what He said. When you give money into the work of God, you're doing something for yourself, and I don't mean just for when you get to Heaven. Certainly, our giving will be rewarded when we get to Heaven, but, believe me, when you get to Heaven, you won't need any extra money! Everything in Heaven is free.

Paul said that no church communicated with him as concerning *giving and receiving*. He was talking about giving and receiving on the earth. If you do the *giving* while you're down here on the earth, why wouldn't the *receiving* be done while you're down here as well. When you study all the references in the Scripture on the subject, the receiving is always while we're here on the earth. People need to expect to receive when they give. In fact, you could say that the Bible never teaches giving. It teaches giving *with receiving* — every single time!

Jesus mentioned this same heavenly banking system in the story of the rich young ruler. When Peter realized that he had done what Jesus had asked that rich young ruler to do — to give — he asked Jesus what he was going to get out of it. Jesus said he would receive "an hundredfold *now in this time*" (Mark 10:30)!

Read carefully the following passage.

MARK 10:17-31
17 And when he [Jesus] **was gone forth into the way, there came one running, and kneeled to him, and asked him, Good Master, what shall I do that I may inherit eternal life?**
18 And Jesus said unto him, Why callest thou me good? there is none good but one, that is, God.
19 Thou knowest the commandments, Do not commit adultery, Do not kill, Do not steal, Do not bear false witness, Defraud not, Honour thy father and mother.
20 And he answered and said unto him, Master, all these have I observed from my youth.
21 Then Jesus beholding him loved him, and said unto him, One thing thou lackest: go thy way, sell whatso-

ever thou hast, and give to the poor, AND THOU SHALT HAVE TREASURE IN HEAVEN: and come, take up the cross, and follow me.
22 And he was sad at that saying, and went away grieved: for he had great possessions.
23 And Jesus looked round about, and saith unto his disciples, How hardly shall they that have riches enter into the kingdom of God!
24 And the disciples were astonished at his words. But Jesus answereth again, and saith unto them, Children, how hard is it for them that trust in riches to enter into the kingdom of God!
25 It is easier for a camel to go through the eye of a needle, than for a rich man to enter into the kingdom of God.
26 And they were astonished out of measure, saying among themselves, Who then can be saved?
27 And Jesus looking upon them saith, With men it is impossible, but not with God: for with God all things are possible.
28 Then Peter began to say unto him, Lo, we have left all, and have followed thee.
29 And Jesus answered and said, Verily I say unto you, There is no man that hath left house, or brethren, or sisters, or father, or mother, or wife, or children, or lands, for my sake, and the gospel's,
30 But he shall receive an hundredfold NOW IN THIS TIME, houses, and brethren, and sisters, and mothers, and children, and lands, with persecutions; and in the world to come eternal life.
31 But many that are first shall be last; and the last first.

This passage of Scripture is packed full of revelation. Many of the questions people have about money are answered right here.

First of all, did you notice that Jesus told this rich young ruler that when he gave to the poor that he would have treasure in Heaven (v. 21). Many people misquote that scripture by leaving that one little phrase out, but that one little phrase is a major revelation that the Body of Christ needs to get in these last days. When we give, we're putting money into our heavenly bank account so God can multiply our investment and return it to us.

You don't need to be ashamed to expect to receive "now in this time" — while you're here on the earth. When you walk into a bank, you're not ashamed to make a withdrawal from your own account, are you? Well, similarly, the harvest off the money you give to God is yours as much as the earnings off money you invest in a CD are yours when it matures. So don't be bashful about your heavenly bank account — just walk in and make your withdrawal!

Some have taught that the cross that Jesus asked this man to bear was to take a vow of poverty and live poor for the rest of his life. Nothing could be further from the truth! As I said, when Peter realized that he had done what Jesus had asked the rich young ruler to do, he asked Jesus what he was going to get out of all he had given up. Jesus said there is no man (that would include the rich young ruler) who left those things for the Gospel's sake who wouldn't receive a hundredfold *now in this time*! Glory to God! In other words, that rich young ruler would have become a *richer young preacher of the Gospel* had he obeyed Jesus' instructions.

This rich young ruler is a perfect example of someone who could trust in the world's way of doing things, but not in *God's* system of prosperity. He was so caught up in the world's system that it blinded him to the way God does things.

Don't misunderstand the Lord's words in Matthew 6

when He said not to lay money up for yourselves on earth. He clarified what He meant when He said, "*. . . how hard is it for them that trust in riches to enter into the kingdom of God!*" (Mark 10:24). It wasn't a matter of misplaced *money*; it was a matter of misplaced *faith*. If the Lord makes you wealthy, you are obviously going to have money in the bank. The issue is keeping your faith in His system of prosperity and not in that money when it starts piling up! If your faith remains in Him, you'll be able to do anything He asks you to do with that money at any time — no questions asked.

It really wasn't the rich young ruler's money that the Lord was after. It was his faith and his heart. His heart just happened to be in his money, so in order to get his heart, Jesus asked him for his money. People have done the same thing over relationships, fame, and many other things. They have refused to give their hearts to the Lord because those things occupied their hearts. Where your treasure is, there your heart is also (Matt. 6:21). So don't be surprised if the Lord asks you at times to give an amount of money that requires you to trust Him for the things you need. He wants your heart and your faith. He'll ask you for things that are precious, but He's not taking anything from you. He's looking for a way to get something to you if you'll respond to Him in faith.

I believe that the rich young ruler could have become a New Testament Abraham if he had obeyed Jesus' instructions. God asked Abraham for Isaac (the most precious thing Abraham had). Abraham obeyed and became one of the richest, most blessed men in the Old Testament.

It is more difficult for people who have already obtained great wealth the world's way to enter into God's system of finance than it is for people who don't have much money. I have had pastors of churches tell me over and over again that they have had millionaires join their church who only gave $100 or less within a year's time. They got their money the world's way, and they won't turn that money loose. The reason is, their faith is in the money they have in the bank and not in the money they have laid up in their heavenly bank account. The Bible says to charge these people to stop that way of thinking and to get into God's system of operating financially.

> **1 TIMOTHY 6:17-19**
> **17 Charge them that are rich in this world, that they be not highminded, nor trust in uncertain riches, but in the living God, who giveth us richly all things to enjoy;**
> **18 That they do good, that they be rich in good works, ready to distribute, willing to communicate;**
> **19 LAYING UP IN STORE FOR THEMSELVES A GOOD FOUNDATION AGAINST THE TIME TO COME, that they may lay hold on eternal life.**

Those pastors who have stingy millionaires (or any stingy person, for that matter) in their churches are to charge them to get "ready and willing," and teach them that the money they lay up in their heavenly bank account is more certain than money that is kept in an earthly account. Paul called the money that is in an earthly account "uncertain riches," but the money that he told them to give he called "a good foundation against the time to come," or, in other words, the future.

The moth and rust (that's the curse) cannot corrupt your heavenly bank account, and the thief (the devil) can't steal it! The Lord told me one time, "Jay, if you give money away, the devil can't take it." I like that, don't you? That's certain! We can secure our futures financially, but natural things are never to be our security. We are to keep our faith in God by making Him our source. How do we do that? By putting money into our heavenly bank account on a regular basis and trusting Him for the return. Someone said, "Yes, but if I give it away, I don't have it." No, remember the Word said that when you give, you are doing it for yourself. *It may leave your hand, but it will never leave your life!* Money will always be there when you need it.

I have had pastors tell me that they were believing God for millionaires to come to their church (they meant Christian millionaires). I told them to begin to believe God to raise up millionaires *in* the church among people prospering *God's* way! Those people will be givers.

A Comprehensive Look at Eternal Life

Let's look at one more thing concerning the rich young ruler. Notice that he came to Jesus and asked what he should do to inherit eternal life (Mark 10:17). Notice again that First Timothy 6:17 charged the rich to lay hold of eternal life.

What is eternal life in these references? It can't be the New Birth or simply going to Heaven. If eternal life did mean that, then Jesus gave that rich young ruler the wrong answer when the young man asked how to obtain it. And in First Timothy 6:17, the people Paul was talking to were already saved.

Eternal life is not just the New Birth. The New Birth is only the doorway in. The term "eternal life" is used in a broad sense in the Scriptures and means *the God kind of life*. It is called, *life*, *abundant life*, *eternal life,* and *the life of God*. In other words, eternal life is not only a *quantity* of life (eternal), but a *quality* of life (abundant). That life includes peace in your mind, harmony in your home and family relationships, health, the joy of the Lord, protection, the favor of God, the witness of the Spirit, and every other blessing in the New Covenant, including financial blessings. Eternal life can be experienced right down here on the earth because the Bible said, *"He that believeth on the Son HATH everlasting life. . . "* (John 3:36).

It is interesting that the rich young ruler had money, but wasn't satisfied with the quality of life that he was living. He obviously knew that he was missing something when he asked Jesus how to obtain the God-quality of life. It's also interesting that the rich folks addressed in First Timothy 6 weren't experiencing that life, although they were born again.

Again, I don't believe the rich young ruler was asking Jesus how to be born again because of Jesus' answer: *". . . go thy way, sell whatsoever thou hast, and give to the poor, and thou shalt have treasure in heaven: and come, take up the cross, and follow me"* (Mark 10:21). You can't earn the New Birth by keeping the commandments or giving money away. Certainly, Jesus was wanting to lead him into the New Birth, but, actually, the New Birth wasn't available yet for Jesus to give. The New Birth was only available after Jesus' blood had been shed, and He was raised from the dead. So what was the issue in these scriptures?

Later, when the man turned away, Jesus said to His disciples, *". . . how hard is it for them that trust in riches to enter into the kingdom of God!"* (Mark 10:24).

What is the Kingdom of God? It is a larger subject than we have time to talk about, but in the context of this scripture and others — talking about money — what does the Kingdom of God mean?

Think about the following scripture.

MATTHEW 6:31-33
31 Therefore take no thought, saying, What shall we eat? or, What shall we drink? or, Wherewithal shall we be clothed?
32 (For after all these things do the Gentiles seek:) for your heavenly Father knoweth that ye have need of all these things.
33 But seek ye first the KINGDOM OF GOD, and his righteousness; and all these things shall be added unto you.

Not only is the Kingdom of God the entire realm of God's dominion, but, as you can see from the context of this scripture, it is *His way of doing things*. Did you notice that this verse contrasts the *way* of the heathen with the *way* of God?

In other words, in order to live in the God-quality of life, you must enter into the Kingdom of God, which is God's way of doing things. This verse contrasts a life consumed with worry to a life consumed with giving to God. Living worry-free is part of the God-kind of life, but if you think about it, living worry-free is not only a superior quality of life, it's also a superior *way* of living.

To Get or To Give?

The entire goal of ungodly men is to gain wealth in any manner they can obtain it. They worry, fuss, devise schemes, even beat one another out of contracts if it means more money to them. According to the statements of Jesus, we're not to go about obtaining wealth in that manner. The world's goal is to see how much they can *get*; our goal is to see how much we can *give*. They live by *getting*; we live by our *giving*.

The context here is obviously money, isn't it? So when Jesus said to seek first the Kingdom of God, He meant *with our money*. God is certainly to be first in every area of our lives, but He is to be our priority financially. Did you notice the very last verse of the passage in Mark 10 about the rich young ruler?

MARK 10:31
31 But many that are first shall be last; and the last first.

The heathen go about to put themselves first financially, but we are to put God first with our giving. As a result of giving, all the things that we need will be added to us. It's the law of sowing and reaping, which is one of God's banking regulations. I like to read Mark 10:31 this way: "Many that put themselves first financially will be the last to get into divine prosperity, and many who put themselves last (after God) financially will be the first to enter into divine prosperity."

Can you see why the masses aren't entering into a financial covenant with God? It's easy to say God is first, but you really find out if He is when you look in your checkbook. When was the last time that you said to yourself or your spouse, "Let's not make that purchase right now because we wouldn't be able to give that thousand dollars to the church that we wanted to give"? Many people have said things, such as, "I can't give right now because I want to do such-and-such for myself," but you seldom hear anyone say, "I can't buy that right now because I want to give such-and-such amount to the Kingdom of God." Putting your giving first will enable you to give like you want to *and* get everything you want also. It's not an "either-or" proposition in the long run.

As I said, the Kingdom of God is God's way of doing things. Jesus explained it in Mark 4:26-29.

MARK 4:26-29
26 And he said, So is the kingdom of God, as if a man should cast seed into the ground;
27 And should sleep, and rise night and day, and the seed should spring and grow up, he knoweth not how.
28 For the earth bringeth forth fruit of herself; first the blade, then the ear, after that the full corn in the ear.
29 But when the fruit is brought forth, immediately he putteth in the sickle, because the harvest is come.

Sowing and reaping is the way the Kingdom of God operates. Faith is the key to the whole thing, because it takes faith to give, and it takes faith to receive. These are the arrangements that God has made for prospering you. Those "arrangements" can take you as far as you're willing to go. It's not in God's character to put a ceiling on how blessed you can be. Why don't you wean yourself off depending on the world's way of doing things? It's so dull and monotonous, anyway.

Why don't you lean back into the Word of God and make a quality decision that you're going to do things God's way and soar upon the heights of possibility that are out there for those who do. There will always be limits on how much you can prosper if you're only operating in natural principles of prosperity. But if you get into *God's* way of prospering and learn to sow seeds toward the things that you and your family need or want, your only limit is how much you can believe for.

Establish the fact right now that no matter what persecution or affliction Satan brings against you, you are going to *give* for a living. No longer will you allow circumstances to dictate whether or not you obey God in your giving. You're going to lay some money up in your heavenly bank account and supersede the limits of this world's system.

Chapter 6
The Prosperity Test

Many have not realized that if you want God's power involved in your money, you have to walk in His way of doing things. A lack of power in this area is simply a lack of submission and obedience to Him in giving. Many times, the things that are highly esteemed among men in this area are an abomination to God (Luke 16:15).

The Hindrance of Pride

For example, when people do things their way, they are able to boast about it. They can say, "My momma and daddy never had anything, but I pulled myself up by my own bootstraps. I'm a self-made man. I worked hard, and I used my head to get where I am today." That kind of attitude stinks in the nostrils of God. To Him it's just stinking, ugly pride. God wants to do things in your life in such a way that *He* gets all the glory.

When things happen in your life that are undeniably the work of God, you have to say, "God did it!" Pride is a major hindrance to your prosperity. We have already seen that grace is a major factor in prospering God's way, but we must also know that He gives his grace to the *humble*.

JAMES 4:6,10
6 But he giveth more grace. Wherefore he saith, God resisteth the proud, but giveth grace unto the humble....
10 Humble yourselves in the sight of the Lord, and he shall lift you up.

When we read these two verses together, we see that it is His grace that lifts us up. Of course, there are many ways that God lifts a person up. For example, being healed by divine power is called being lifted up (James 5:14,15). But we have already found that there is grace to prosper us, so when God prospers us by His grace, we are being lifted up. We have also learned that we release our faith to receive this grace by our giving. Now notice the following verses.

PSALM 113:7,8
7 He RAISETH UP the poor out of the dust, and LIFTETH the needy out of the dunghill;
8 That he may set him with princes, even with the princes of his people.

These verses tell us that when God gets His power involved in your money, His power is going to lift you up high above poverty. Glory to God! Deuteronomy 28:13 also tells us that God will lift you so high financially that you will be *above only*! That means that you won't ever be close to poverty again. That's pretty high!

The 'Manure Pile' of Poverty

Did you notice what God said it was like when people live in poverty? He said it was like living in a manure pile or "dunghill" (Ps. 113:7). If there is a manure pile around, you stay as far away from it as possible, don't you?

Well, God wants to get you as far away from the manure pile of poverty as you'll let Him. He wants to lift you way above it. Someone said, "Well, believe me — I'll let Him!" It's one thing to say that, but it's another thing entirely to actually let Him do it. According to the Word, it requires humbling oneself to God's way of doing things in order for this kind of power to be on you.

Humility: The Great Qualifier For Being Lifted Up By God

Some have thought that it is wrong to be lifted up. No, God is telling us that He *wants* to lift us up. The problem comes when we lift ourselves up our own way. God wants to lift us up by His power, and He wants to do it His way. If we get impatient with Him, we only delay qualifying ourselves for greater prosperity.

The 'Humility Test'

Humility is a valuable commodity to God and is a prerequisite to prosperity. If one won't humble himself to God's method of prosperity and His way of doing things, he disqualifies himself from ever receiving God's help. There are tests to pass in order to experience the kind of prospering that lifts you to the place of being "above only." If you don't know what the tests are, you'll not ever know if you qualify for more prosperity.

Many times when the Bible speaks of testing, it is referring to the enemy trying us with affliction or persecution (Mark 4:17; 1 Thess. 3:1-5; James 1:1-17). But God is not one to put bad things on you in order to test you. To begin with, He doesn't have any bad things up in Heaven to put on us. If He used things like tragedy, sickness, or poverty to test us or make us humble, He would have to get in league with the devil, and He doesn't do that.

When I say there is a test to pass in order to break into new levels of prosperity, I'm not referring to what the devil does in your life. I'm talking about what the Bible says in Luke 16:10 and 12.

> **LUKE 16:10,12**
> **10 He that is faithful in that which is least is faithful also in much: and he that is unjust in the least is unjust also in much. . . .**
> **12 And if ye have not been faithful in that which is another man's** [*The Amplified Bible* says, "whether God's or man's]**, who shall give you that which is your own?**

Once again, the context of these verses is money. We know that the tithe belongs to God, so Jesus is talking to us about our faithfulness in giving tithes *and* offerings. One way we could interpret these verses is, if we're not obedient in giving our tithes and offerings, we can't be trusted in any other area in which God wants to use us.

Money is the least of things to be counted faithful in. If you're not faithful to God with your money, how can He trust you with greater power to prosper — or with the healing anointing or *any* of the things of the Spirit?

If you want God to use you to raise up a great work for Him, your faithfulness to Him with your money is the greatest indicator to Him as to whether you can be trusted. If you won't obey Him when He tells you to give Him your last $500, you can't be trusted with the anointing to prosper. You just won't get this kind of power working for you, causing you to prosper, until you can be trusted to obey God with money.

There are tests all along the road to prosperity that you'll have to pass to get to the next level. Not everyone qualifies to have this kind of power on him to prosper. It can destroy a person if he doesn't know how to handle money.

Every believer goes through the same faith school in receiving their prosperity from God. The Bible tells us that the things that happened to the Israelites in the Old Testament happened to them as types (1 Cor. 10:11). Israel went from the land of "not enough" (slavery) to "just enough" (in the wilderness) to "more than enough" (in Canaan's land). Each time they had to obey God to get to the next level. The same is true for you and me today. In order to move out of the land of "not enough" or "just enough," we must take the appropriate steps of faith.

One thing we must be completely convinced of is that it is the perfect will of God for every believer to live in the land of more than enough. He is no respecter of persons (Acts 10:34). Jesus made prosperity available to all of us by His grace when He became poor that we might be rich (2 Cor. 8:9).

To Humility, We Must Add Faith

The word "rich" means *abundance* or *more than one needs*. However, our prospering is not only a matter of what God has done for us, but a matter of our obedience and our faith. The reason the Israelites wandered in the wilderness for forty years was because they wouldn't submit to God's way of getting them into Canaan's land — by obeying what God had told them to do.

The 'Giving Test'

Many people focus on the sending end (God's end) when they need more money. But if we are constantly living without, the problem is not on the sending end but on our end or, we could say, the *receiving* end. The first place we should look is at our faithfulness to see if we have been faithful to the Lord in our giving. You can readily see from Luke 16:10 and 12 that there is a "giving test" that must be passed before we are able to move on to the next level of increase. God is looking for faithfulness with what we have right now.

When God speaks to us to give, we are being proven or tested. Our response to Him determines if we qualify for greater prosperity. We can respond in faith and obey, or we can respond in unbelief and disobey.

In the past, the Church has thought that God tests us through trouble or hardship. No, Satan tries us with trouble and hardship (affliction, poverty, and so forth) to destroy us (1 Thess. 3:1-5; Mark 4:17; John 10:10). God tries our hearts, but He does it with His Word, not affliction or poverty. His goal is to elevate us into greater levels of blessing.

> **PROVERBS 17:3**
> **3 The fining pot is for silver, and the furnace for gold: but THE LORD TRIETH THE HEARTS.**

The Lord is looking for an obedient heart. When He speaks to you to give in an offering, He's watching to see if you will obey Him. When you prove to Him that you will obey Him with your money, He can trust you with greater anointing to prosper. God doesn't necessarily give you more money, He gives you more power to get the money (Deut.

8:18). He gives you more grace (2 Cor. 9:8). He increases your revelation and your faith (Rom. 1:17).

Notice that James 4:6 starts out by saying, *"He giveth MORE GRACE...."* More of God's power and favor on you mixed with greater faith will move you into greater prosperity!

Many want to be in a place where they are managing hundreds of thousands of dollars, but they have never learned to manage a hundred-dollar bill when God deals with them to give it. God's system just doesn't work that way. If you want to prosper, you're going to have to obey God when He talks to you, and if you want more prosperity, you're going to have to obey God when He tells you to give bigger.

Two Kinds of Unbelief

There are two kinds of unbelief mentioned in the Bible. First, there is the kind of unbelief that comes because someone doesn't know what God has said about a certain subject. You cannot believe beyond actual knowledge.

For example, if you don't know that it is God's will to prosper you, it would be impossible for you to believe God for prosperity. Faith begins where the will of God is known.

A good example of this kind of unbelief is found in Acts 19:1-7.

ACTS 19:1-7
1 And it came to pass, that, while Apollos was at Corinth, Paul having passed through the upper coasts came to Ephesus: and finding certain disciples,
2 He said unto them, Have ye received the Holy Ghost since ye believed? And they said unto him, We have not so much as heard whether there be any Holy Ghost.

3 And he said unto them, Unto what then were ye baptized? And they said, Unto John's baptism.
4 Then said Paul, John verily baptized with the baptism of repentance, saying unto the people, that they should believe on him which should come after him, that is, on Christ Jesus.
5 When they heard this, they were baptized in the name of the Lord Jesus.
6 And when Paul had laid his hands upon them, the Holy Ghost came on them; and they spake with tongues, and prophesied.
7 And all the men were about twelve.

These men had never heard about the baptism of the Holy Ghost, so it was impossible for them to receive this experience. The Bible says that faith comes by hearing, and hearing by the Word of God (Rom. 10:17). In order to get these men out of unbelief, Paul had to tell them about Jesus and the Holy Ghost.

The *second* kind of unbelief is *unpersuadableness* or *disobedience*. Once someone hears the Word, he must allow it to take precedence over everything else that he knows, and he must walk in obedience to it.

This second kind of unbelief was the kind that kept the children of Israel out of the land of abundance. They would not allow the Word of God to persuade them that they had been given all the wealth of Canaan's land. They allowed the report of the ten spies to take precedence over what God had said (*see* Numbers 13:17-33). As a result, they ended up disobeying God and not going in and possessing their God-given blessings. Their disobedience caused them to fail the prosperity test.

Possessing New Territories

Many have not realized that when they disobey God's leadings in their giving, they are failing the prosperity test. When we give in obedience to the Word and the Holy Ghost, we are *possessing* new territories of abundance. If we disobey, we end up wandering around in the same wilderness of lack year after year.

God didn't put the children of Israel in the wilderness for forty years. They put *themselves* there through their disobedience. They tell us that it was only an eleven-day trip from the Red Sea to Kadesh Barnea. If they had obeyed God, they could have been living in Canaan's blessings right away. As it was, they went to "faith school" for forty years in the wilderness in order to learn how to possess the land!

Many have misunderstood what was happening out in the wilderness. They think that God only sent them out there to judge them. The Bible says that He also took them out there to teach them how to possess the land of Canaan. Notice Deuteronomy 8:3 and 16.

> **DEUTERONOMY 8:3,16**
> **3 And he humbled thee, and suffered thee to hunger, and fed thee with manna, which thou knewest not, neither did thy fathers know; that he might MAKE THEE KNOW that man doth not live by bread only, but by every word that proceedeth out of the mouth of the Lord doth man live....**
> **16 Who fed thee in the wilderness with manna, which thy fathers knew not, that he might HUMBLE THEE, and that he might PROVE THEE, TO DO THEE GOOD AT THY LATTER END.**

Can you see that God was using the situation to train them to live by faith? No, God didn't put them in the position of lack that they were in. They put themselves there through disobedience. But God took advantage of the situation and began preparing them for greater things.

You might ask, "What do you mean by that?" These verses in Deuteronomy said that God taught them to live by the words that came out His mouth so that He could do them good in the end. The good that He was talking about was Canaan's land. In other words, the whole time they were out there, God was pointing them in the direction of abundance. He still had Canaan's land on His mind the whole time they were out there. When He gave them manna out of the sky to eat, they were being trained to live by faith, because it was going to require faith on their part to go into the greater blessings of God!

You learn to live by faith when you're living from day to day financially. No, it's not the perfect will of God, but you need to take advantage of those times and exercise your faith for food on your table by giving right in the middle of those times of lack. Rather than complain about the hardships, you need to make the most of the opportunity to develop your faith. If you grumble and refuse to give when the devil throws his junk at you, you're failing the test. However, when you continue to tithe and give regardless of the circumstances, you're taking your first step toward possessing the land.

Let's look a little bit more at how God tests us with His Word.

> **PSALM 105:19**
> **19 Until the time that his word came: the word of the Lord tried him** [talking about Joseph]**.**

This verse is speaking of the word that God gave to Joseph about him ruling over his brothers. Most people know the story. There were many things that happened that could have made Joseph give up on the word from God, but Joseph kept true to the promise of God, and the dream finally came to pass in grand style just as God had promised.

Many people would have given up about the time Joseph was sold into slavery. Most everyone else would have quit the Word and given up when Potiphar had Joseph thrown into jail or when the chief butler forgot to put in a good word to the pharaoh for him. We've all heard those kinds of people talk: "I've tried that faith business. It just doesn't work for everybody." The truth is, they didn't try the Word; the Word tried *them*, and they flunked the test, so they're back in spiritual kindergarten.

There is a faith school that every Christian must go through. I've heard people say, "Well, I don't believe that we can all be rich. After all, Jesus said, 'Give us this day our daily bread.' So all I'm asking for is to have enough to get by on from day to day. After all, didn't God tell the Israelites not to gather more than one day's supply of manna in the wilderness?"

Yes, that's true, but the children of Israel were in faith school learning to live by faith!

You see, you have to start out where you are in faith. If you are at the day-to-day level of faith, then that's where you have to start out. If you pass the giving test on that level, you can get into the land of more than enough!

Every step of the way, just understand that God is teaching you to walk by His Word and to make Him your source so that He can take you into greater prosperity. When Jesus said, "Give us this day our daily bread, He wasn't saying that "day to day" is all that is available to us. To come to that conclusion would contradict many other things He said. No, Jesus was saying, "Give us this day our daily bread," because that's where you start out. Once you learn to believe God on that level, you can go on to the next level or grade in faith school.

If you are a student of the Word of God concerning prosperity, you know that God takes you into prosperity step-by-step according to your faith. Jesus said divine prosperity is like planting seed into the earth. The seed brings forth *". . . first the blade, then the ear, after that the full corn in the ear"* (Mark 4:28). And Paul called God the God of *increase* (1 Cor. 3:6,7).

Psalm 115:14 says, *"The Lord shall increase you MORE AND MORE, you and your children."*

The principle of increase is illustrated throughout the Bible. For example, David took the opportunity to use his faith on the lion and the bear before he ever killed a giant. It would be good for you to get some experience under your belt before you go after the giants too! David wasn't out there just loafing off while he was keeping those sheep. He was evidently using his time to meditate in the Word of God, because that's what he was full of when the circumstances of life came against him.

We grow in faith just like we grow naturally. The way you grow in faith is through meditating in the Word of God and acting upon it. When you act upon God's Word, you are putting it to the test and proving it to be true. Once you've gotten some experience under your belt, you'll begin to expect God to come through for you exactly as He did the last time (*see* Romans 5:4 and 5).

One thing we must realize is, not only are we to prove

the Word out, but that the Word will prove *us* out too. Once again, Psalm 105:19 says, *"Until the time that his word came: the word of the Lord TRIED HIM."* The word translated "tried" here means *to test by experiment in order to prove to be true*; *to authenticate, substantiate, certify, validate, or confirm*.

Most of the time, we only think of testing in the negative sense. God is not a negative God. He is a *faith* God! He believes in us. He doesn't give us His Word to disqualify us and to keep us from the blessing when we don't believe and obey it. He gives us His Word to prove to the devil that we will obey Him and so that He can legally make good on His Word when we do. The devil can't do a thing about our blessing when we stay loyal to God's Word, and God can just laugh in the devil's face and go ahead and bless us.

God will often talk to you about giving something away in order to certify your faith for greater blessings financially. When we understand this, we'll understand a very religious verse.

GENESIS 22:1,2
1 And it came to pass after these things, that God did tempt Abraham, and SAID UNTO HIM [notice He tempted Abraham with His Word, not with affliction or poverty], Abraham: and he said, Behold, here I am.
2 And he SAID, Take now thy son, thine only son Isaac, whom thou lovest, and get thee into the land of Moriah; and offer him there for a burnt offering upon one of the mountains which I will tell thee of.

God didn't tempt (certify) Abraham because He didn't know if Abraham would obey Him or not. God had already said He knew Abraham and that He knew

Abraham would obey Him (Gen. 18:19). God was simply giving Abraham an opportunity to pass the test and certify his faith and be blessed in a greater way.

In Genesis 12:1-3, we read that God had already told Abraham that He would bless and multiply him. But after Abraham obeyed God and gave part of that blessing (Isaac) back to Him, God said to Abraham, "*. . . IN BLESSING I will BLESS thee, and IN MULTIPLYING I will MULTIPLY thy seed as the stars of the heaven, and as the sand which is upon the sea shore; and thy seed shall possess the gate of his enemies*" (Gen. 22:17).

In other words, God was saying to Abraham, "While I'm blessing you, I'm going to bless you, and while I'm multiplying you, I'm going to multiply you"!

Abraham was already a tither at this time (Gen. 14:17-24) and was experiencing the blessing. But he got a greater blessing out of his offerings — his giving. The same is true for us today. I believe that there is a blessing upon those who tithe but that there is an *extra special* blessing upon those who obey Him in offerings. Having my money be multiplied is good, but I like it when money multiplies while it's multiplying! Things happen much quicker and bigger when you multiply what has been multiplied. If that is happening in your finances, it will propel you quickly into the land of more than enough.

Let's not let the Lord find our hearts wanting in faith when He speaks to us to give. God believes in us. He's pulling for us; He's on our side. He's expecting us to obey and prove out that the Word is true. When God told us to prove Him with our tithes and offerings in Malachi 3:10, He didn't mean to try tithing and see if it works. That would be unbelief. He said to *prove* that He will bless us by obeying the Word in faith.

Malachi 3:13 and 14 go on to say that when you bring your tithes and offerings, make your mouth do its duty.

MALACHI 3:13,14
13 Your words have been stout against me, saith the Lord. Yet ye say, What have we spoken so much against thee?
14 Ye have said, It is vain to serve God: and what profit is it that we have kept his ordinance, and that we have walked mournfully before the Lord of hosts?

In other words, when you obey God and His Word in tithes and offerings, say, "This is profiting me greatly. I'm bringing my tithes and offerings to the Lord, and He is opening the windows of Heaven on me and pouring me out a blessing that there is not room enough to receive.

"God is proving to me that He is faithful to His Word. He said that the devourer is rebuked for me [Mal. 3:11], so I say that Satan has no power over my money to take it away from me. Money is coming to me everywhere I go. I'm expecting checks in the mail and favor with every person that I do business with. I'm on top because Satan is under my feet. I can't fail because I'm acting on God's Word, and His Word can't fail."

When you're still saying things such as that weeks later when your faith's confession doesn't look like it's working, you're passing the faith test. When you stay on God's side and don't side against the Word by confessing the wrong thing, you're passing the faith test. *Tithing and giving are not complete until you make the right confession of faith!*

Deuteronomy 26 is a good passage of Scripture on tithing, and it also bears witness to that fact. Three separate times in this chapter (vv. 3,5,13), God told them to make a confession of His blessings on them while they were tithing. On top of that, He told them to worship Him and rejoice in all His blessings (vv. 10,11). You may not see many of the blessings yet that came on you when you began to tithe and give, but you can begin to worship Him anyway. The Bible tells us that faith calls things that be not as though they were (Rom. 4:17).

As you and I begin to praise God in advance for His blessings on us, we are completing our tithing and giving with our faith. When we talk about how big the need is and how hard it is to get ahead, we're failing the faith test, and in doing that, we end up never really completing our tithing or giving. We abort our blessing before it is ever born if we fail to understand and pass God's prosperity test.

Chapter 7
The Candle of the Lord

Have you ever been in strife with the Lord over the amount He told you to give in an offering? "That just can't be the Lord," you said to yourself. "After all, He doesn't want me to be foolish." That is true; God doesn't want you to be foolish. But if it *is* Him telling you to give, it would be foolish to hold on to that money.

There is often a battle between your head and your heart at times like this. The whole time you are arguing with the Lord about what He is asking you to do, your spirit is siding in *with* the Lord, *against* you — your flesh or what your mind is telling you. Your spirit man is excited about what it heard the Lord say. In fact, you almost laughed right out loud when you heard the Lord speak to you, because, for one split second, you "saw" how obeying what He told you to do would release you from that problem you've been having getting your bills paid on time.

But about that time, your head threw a shroud of darkness over your excitement. *How am I going to pay all these bills if I give this money away?* you thought. So you dismissed what you had in your heart, deciding that what you "heard" God say really wasn't God at all.

If this has ever happened to you, welcome to the first grade of faith school! Your head really can't see what the spirit man can, because the Lord doesn't speak to your head, He speaks to your spirit man. The things of the spirit can only be spiritually understood.

1 CORINTHIANS 2:14
14 But the natural man receiveth not the things of the Spirit of God: for they are foolishness unto him: neither can he know them, because they are spiritually discerned.

If we operate out of the revelation we have in our spirit, and "bring our head along for the ride," our head will eventually "see" that giving that money was the smartest thing we ever did. You see, you're head doesn't know the future, but God (who dwells in your spirit) knows the future better than *you* know the *past*. When He inspires you to give, particularly when He tells you to give in an unusually big way, He is preparing you for a harvest that you're going to need in the future.

Illumination in Your Spirit Can Put You Over in Financial Difficulties

The Lord has spoken to me quite a lot recently about the candle of the Lord in relation to these kinds of leadings in our giving. Let's notice some scriptures that mention it.

PROVERBS 20:27
27 The spirit of man is the candle of the Lord, searching all the inward parts of the belly.

This verse establishes right off the bat what the candle of the Lord is. It is our spirit man. Now in order to determine which part of man He is talking about when He refers to the spirit man, we must know that man is a three-part being.

1 THESSALONIANS 5:23
23 And the very God of peace sanctify you wholly; and

> **I pray God your whole SPIRIT and SOUL and BODY be preserved blameless unto the coming of our Lord Jesus Christ.**

In this passage, the Apostle Paul by the unction of the Spirit tells us that man is a three-part being. This simply lets us know that there is a difference between the soul and spirit of man, just as there is a difference between the soul and *body* of man. The soul and spirit of man are no more one and the same than the soul and body are one and the same.

With our bodies, we contact this physical realm; with our souls (mind, will, and emotions), we contact the mental realm; and with our spirits, we contact the Spirit realm. For this reason, it is possible for our spirit man to know things that our mind doesn't know, because he is in contact with the Spirit of God, and our minds are not.

Proverbs 20:27 is telling us that when God illuminates us, He does it in our spirit. Since the natural man cannot receive the things of the Spirit of God, the natural man will many times fight the spirit man for control. If he wins, you lose! But if you walk in the light of what comes into your spirit and resist the attempts of your mind to put out the light, you'll step out of the natural and over into the realm of the supernatural! Glory to God! Operating out of your spirit will bring forth the move of God that you are looking for in your finances!

The Role of Walking in the Light Of Your Spirit in Sowing and Reaping

Now let's notice something Jesus said right in the middle of one of the greatest chapters in the Bible about sowing and reaping — Mark chapter 4.

MARK 4:21,22
21 And he said unto them, Is a CANDLE brought to be put under a bushel, or under a bed? and not to be set on a candlestick?
22 For there is nothing hid, which shall not be manifested; neither was any thing kept secret, but that it should come abroad.

The context of these verses is Jesus' teachings on the law of sowing and reaping. In the preceding verses, Jesus taught us the parable of the sower sowing the Word, and in a following verse, Jesus said, "*. . . So is the kingdom of God, as if a man should cast seed into the ground*" (v. 26) and went on to give us two more parables on the law of sowing and reaping.

So what is Jesus telling us when He begins to talk about the candle of the Lord right in the middle of His teachings on sowing and reaping? By rules of Bible interpretation, unless it specifically tells us otherwise, we must interpret the word "candle" to mean the same thing in this verse as other Bible verses containing the word. *Jesus is telling us that the Spirit of God doesn't illuminate us in our spirits by His Word just so we can put out the light and continue to walk in our own reasoning!*

God Doesn't Want You To Stumble In the Darkness Financially

In our day, we have light bulbs to give us light. We don't turn on the light in a room and then go throw a heavy blanket over it so we can stumble around in the dark. We turn on the light so we can see where we're going.

In the same way, we shouldn't put out the light that comes into our spirit with the shroud of reasoning. We're not supposed to walk as mere unregenerate men in the vanity of our mind. We're not supposed to "figure everything out." If you try to figure out how to fix the mess you're in, you're going to get "brain lock"! You need to get out of your mind and into your spirit. That's where the real answers to your problems are.

This is certainly true about walking in the light of the Word in the midst of *any* kind of crisis in life. But our head will fight the Word in times of financial crisis in particular, because the unrenewed mind can't figure out how giving money away will help us get *ahead*. That just doesn't compute in your mind's way of looking at things.

Let's look at another passage of Scripture along this line.

> **LUKE 11:33-36**
> **33 No man, when he hath LIGHTED A CANDLE, putteth it in a secret place, neither under a bushel, but on a candlestick, that they which come in may see the light.**
> **34 The light of the body is the eye: therefore when thine eye is single [or healthy or clear], thy whole body also is full of light; but when thine eye is evil [or unhealthy], thy body also is full of darkness.**
> **35 Take heed therefore that the light which is in thee be not darkness.**
> **36 If thy whole body therefore be full of light, having no part dark, the whole shall be full of light, AS WHEN THE BRIGHT SHINING OF A CANDLE DOTH GIVE THEE LIGHT.**

In this passage of Scripture, Jesus once again illustrates what He is talking about by using natural light as an example. He said that if your eye can see, then your whole body will be full of light. In other words, if your *eye* can't see then your *foot* won't be able to either! In other words, your foot may get stumped on the bedpost!

Now your foot can't literally see, but if it will allow the eye to control it with respect to what it sees, that foot will be able to "see" the bedpost and avoid running into it. Your foot has to rely on what your eye sees. If the foot would trust what the eye sees, it won't get black and blue so often.

Your Mind Must Defer to Your Spirit

The same is true concerning the light that comes into your spirit — the candle of the Lord. God illuminates us in our spirit so that He can enlighten our mind. The mind really can't "see" what the spirit man does when God speaks to us to give, but if the mind will allow the spirit to control it with respect to what it sees, the mind will "see" and be able to move away from that financial problem.

If you will allow yourself to be governed by the light that comes into your spirit, your finances won't get "black and blue" so often. The more mental gymnastics of worry you go through trying to fix a financial problem, the more entangled you will get. You'll begin to think that your problem is a complex ball of confusion. But if you'll lay down your own attempts to fix your problem in the flesh, and walk in the light of what God is showing you in your spirit, you'll begin to see just how simple the problem really is. Revelation makes things simple, but darkness tends to make things complicated.

Your Problems Are Simple To Solve!

Paul told the Corinthians, *"...I fear, lest by any means, as the serpent beguiled Eve through his subtilty* [craftiness], *so your MINDS should be corrupted from the SIMPLICITY that is in Christ"* (2 Cor. 11:3).

You need to make a regular confession that, "This problem is *simple*!" It really *is* when you have light.

Have you ever stumbled around in the dark trying to find something because you didn't want to take the time to turn on the light? You got more confused the farther you went, didn't you? Not only did you not find what you were looking for, you created more confusion every time you bumped into something you didn't know was there. "What is that?" you found yourself saying, and then it took you a minute to feel around for "where it went," so you wouldn't hurt yourself!

"Oh, that's the chair. Well, what is it doing over here?" Then you try to figure out where you really are because "that chair doesn't belong over here." In the meantime, you find out that the chair really is in the right place — *you* just weren't where you thought *you* were! If you would have just taken the time to turn on the light, your problems wouldn't have seemed so complex.

Paul was telling us in Second Corinthians 11:3 that Satan makes things complex in our minds. But, thank God, when we govern our minds by the light of the Word of God that came into our spirit, things become easy again. You can really tell how much unbelief you are in by how hard things are to you. God wants you to have "simple" childlike faith.

Have you ever noticed that children aren't too complicated? That's the way the Lord wants us to be when it comes to our faith. When He tells us what to do to get out of some financial mess we've gotten ourselves into, let's just walk in the light of what He has said and not play into the devil's trap of thinking that our problem is hard. Let's not put out the candle of the Lord.

If you put out the light in your spirit with the "bushel basket" of reasoning, things are going to get really dark, and you'll become more confused than you ever have been. Walk in the light, and your path will get brighter and brighter, and the blessings of God will overtake you!

Chapter 8
Becoming a Professional Giver

There are several ways people go about obtaining wealth. Some ways require no faith in God whatsoever and are displeasing to the Lord. Some ways require *some* faith; still others require *more* faith. One thing about the Lord is, without faith, it is impossible to please Him (Heb. 11:6), and that includes faith for prosperity as well. The more dependent you are upon God's Word to prosper you, the more pleasing you'll be to the Lord, and the greater your blessings will be.

Notice three ways you can go about obtaining money.

Some Obtain Money By Stealing

First of all, some steal in order to obtain the things that they need or want. According to the following verse, we are to do away with that method of operating.

> **EPHESIANS 4:28**
> **28 Let him that STOLE STEAL NO MORE: but rather let him LABOUR, WORKING WITH HIS HANDS the thing which is good, that he may have to GIVE TO HIM THAT NEEDETH.**

Most Christians immediately think of unsaved people when someone talks about stealing, but notice that the Apostle Paul was writing this to born-again, Spirit-filled Christians. Would it be possible that Christians would need to be told to stop stealing? It must be, because Paul told some of the Ephesians to stop stealing.

If you want the best God has for you along this line, you're going to have to be totally honest. That means with your employer as well as with God. Stealing is dishonesty and it's sin. According to the Bible, you cannot live in sin and prosper.

PROVERBS 28:13
13 He that covereth his sins shall not prosper: but whoso confesseth and forsaketh them shall have mercy.

There is more to the message of prosperity than just giving and making good confessions. You're going to have to be honest in your business affairs. God is a God of truth, and His Spirit is the Spirit of truth. If you are not acting totally truthful, you're being displeasing to Him, and He can't bless you. If you want the Spirit to come on you to bless and prosper all that you put your hand to, you're going to have to be truthful, because He is the Spirit of truth.

So we must do away with stealing to obtain what we need.

Some Obtain Money By Laboring

The *second* way Ephesians 4:28 mentions that a person may obtain wealth is to work with his hands. Most Christians operate in this area in order to make a living. They get up early, work all day, and come home with their paycheck. They do that because they have bills to pay and little mouths to feed.

This way of operating financially is a level of faith in God that says, "If I work, God will provide my needs, and if

I work harder, God will provide more of what I need and maybe even some of my *wants*." God is a God who will meet you on whatever level you come to Him on, as long as you are walking in all the light you have.

I have found this to be true in ministering to the sick. The younger in the Lord the person is who needs healing, the more the nine manifestations of the gifts of the Spirit will come into operation. I can't count the times that I have come out of a service where I ministered healing to people by the gifts of the Spirit, and the pastor of the church said to me, "Every single person you ministered to tonight was someone I've never seen before. I just talked to some of them, and they are from denominational churches here in the area. You didn't minister to one of my members by the gifts of the Spirit."

I didn't know who his members were, so it couldn't have been me deciding who would receive a manifestation of a gift of the Spirit. The reason the Lord didn't minister to those pastors' people that way was, those pastors had been teaching them the Word of God, and the Lord expected the people to walk in the light of what they knew. Healing was for them as well as for the denominational people, but the Bible-taught believers knew how to appropriate healing by their faith in the Word of God apart from a manifestation of the gifts of the Spirit.

In the same way, God might "wink" and patiently smile at Christians who put their faith in Him on the level of just "working for a living." Now stay with me on this one, or you'll miss what I'm saying. I'm about to say some things that may make you want to throw this book down and declare it to be heresy. But if you'll listen to what I'm about to say, I can help you get into a higher way of believing for prosperity. Hear me out all the way to the end before you judge what I'm saying.

Stay Out of the Ditches — Go Down the Middle of the Road

The Bible does teach that we are to work (1 Thess. 4:11-12) and that He will bless what we put our hands to (Deut. 28:8). But I think we have emphasized that to the point of error. I call it "error by emphasis." That just simply means that we have emphasized the work ethic to the point that people no longer have a *faith* ethic. Don't misunderstand me. Some have pushed this thing too far the other way and have gotten in the ditch on the other side of the road. There is a ditch on both sides of this road, but God wants us to go down the middle of the road and be blessed.

The Faith Ethic

What do I mean by a faith ethic? I mean that working for a living isn't the highest way of operating financially. God will meet you there, but if all you're depending on is your job to prosper you, you have limited Him in a sense, because you're not opening up the door for Him to bless you in any other way than through your job. Your faith needs to be in His *Word* rather than in your job. Your faith needs to be in His *grace* rather than in your work. Your faith needs to be in what He has done for you, not in what you're doing on your job.

Notice again the verse we started out with in this book.

2 CORINTHIANS 8:9
9 For ye know the grace of our Lord Jesus Christ, that, though he was rich, yet for your sakes he became poor, that ye through his poverty might be rich.

This verse didn't say, "Work to be rich." It said, "There is grace to be rich." If Jesus has made you rich by His grace, then why are you working to be rich? Because that's what you were told you had to do to make money!

Let me say again that God will meet you there if that's all you know, but there is a generation of people coming up who are going for the best God has for them, and they have found out that working for a living, trying to get rich, isn't the best He has for them. They're a new breed. They are the final generation who are being equipped through the Word of God with the supernatural. They are the generation who will bring in the harvest of souls from the earth, and God is training them to do everything they do supernaturally, because that's the only way they're going to get the job done.

We're challenging everything we've ever been told to see if those things are really so in the Word of God. The things that are will remain; the things that aren't must go; and the things that aren't the best God has for us are no longer enough! The generations that have gone before were content to stay on a lower level of faith, but we are not. This is the time of the fullness of all things. God is ready to fully manifest the blessing of prosperity, because this is the generation that is requiring it of Him. We must have the fullness of the promises, because we're the generation that must reap the harvest of the souls of the earth.

Some Obtain Money By Giving

What is the best God has for us? Let's look again at Ephesians 4:28.

> **EPHESIANS 4:28**
> **28 Let him that stole steal no more: but rather let him labour, working with his hands the thing which is good, THAT HE MAY HAVE TO GIVE TO HIM THAT NEEDETH.**

The highest way God has for us to make a living and become prosperous is to *give* for it. This verse tells us that we're to work to get money so that we can have seed to sow. Many are working just for a living. That just means they are eating all their income — their seed! But this verse tells us that there is a higher way. According to this verse, we can work for a *giving* and then live off our giving!

"Well, Brother Jay, there's just no way that will work. If I give all my money away, I won't be able to pay my bills." Well, you may not be there in your faith right now, especially if you haven't been feeding your faith and renewing your mind with the Word. But Jesus said, "According to your faith, so be it unto you."

You need to start where you are. First of all, if you're not tithing, then begin there. Did you notice that Ephesians 4:28 started out with tithing. It said, *"Let him that stole steal no more. . . ."* That's in agreement with Malachi 3:8, which says, *"Will a man rob God? Yet ye have robbed me. But ye say, Wherein have we robbed thee? In tithes and offerings."*

You're not even giving until you have brought your tithe to the Lord. Tithing isn't giving. Tithing is returning to the

Lord what is already His. That is the reason the Bible says that if you're not tithing, you're robbing God. You can't rob someone of something that isn't even his.

Then, once you've begun returning the tithes to the Lord, you can begin to give offerings. As your faith grows, you can increase your giving on a percentage basis.

It's not just giving more money that will cause you to be blessed more, especially if your faith isn't there yet. It's the faith that you mix with that seed that will cause a harvest of blessings to come to you. In other words, give in proportion to your faith. Don't do something that causes your faith to stretch beyond where you can really have confidence. That kind of thing will produce no results and has given the faith message a bad name. People have done things that really weren't faith to begin with and ended up in a mess.

Prosperity Is By Grace Through Faith

Just because God can meet all your needs if you give your paycheck away doesn't mean that your faith is there yet. Just like every blessing from God, prosperity is by His grace, but through your faith. In other words, it is your faith that measures out the blessing to you (Mark 4:24).

This truth just brings us back to the fact that God is not a God who likes to limit us. Limits are not from God. The only limits are the ones we place on Him (Ps. 78:41; Matt. 9:29).

Think about this for a moment. If prosperity is a grace, then you can't earn it by what you do. You must receive prosperity by faith. If that is true, then why would we have to give to prosper? Notice Second Corinthians 8:7-9.

2 CORINTHIANS 8:7-9
7 Therefore, as ye abound in every thing, in faith, and utterance, and knowledge, and in all diligence, and in your love to us, SEE THAT YE ABOUND IN THIS GRACE ALSO.
8 I speak not by commandment, but by occasion of the forwardness of others, and to prove the sincerity of your love.
9 For ye know the grace of our Lord Jesus Christ, that, though he was rich, yet for your sakes he became poor, that ye through his poverty might be rich.

From the context, when Paul told the Corinthians to "abound in this grace also," he meant the grace of giving. Then he said for them to give to "prove the sincerity of their love." After he made those statements, he immediately referred them to the fact that it was the Lord's graciousness toward them that had made them rich.

In other words, Paul was telling them to give freely, because prosperity had come to them freely. He told them that giving was a "love" thing to do. Later in his letter to the Corinthians, Paul said something similar on the subject.

2 CORINTHIANS 9:6-8
6 But this I say, He which soweth sparingly shall reap also sparingly; and he which soweth bountifully shall reap also bountifully.
7 Every man according as he purposeth in his heart, so let him give; not grudgingly, or of necessity: for God loveth a cheerful giver.
8 And God is able to make all grace abound toward you; that ye, always having all sufficiency in all things, may abound to every good work:

Once again, the Word of God only mentions God's grace

for prosperity after it mentions giving. I like to illustrate this point by saying, "The pipe that brings the water to your house is always wet." What do I mean? If you will be a channel of God's blessings to others, you will stay blessed yourself.

Galatians 5:6 says that faith works by love. When you apply that to the things we're talking about, it means that your faith for prosperity will only work when you become a giver, because giving is an act of love.

Love is the New Testament commandment (John 13:34), so love is the key to everything else working for you, including your faith for prosperity.

Giving To Get?

If you are a giver, your giving liberates your faith to receive from God. I don't mean that love is the only reason we should give. I have had people tell me, "Well, I just don't believe that we should give to get. I just believe that we should give to people because we love them." That is only partly true. We are to give out of love *and* faith. I mean, we are to give because we love the Lord and His people, but we are also to give because of our faith in God's Word. Why would He tell us that we would reap if He didn't want us to believe for and expect it?

What's really amazing is that some farmers don't believe we should sow money in order to reap a harvest. Well, if they don't believe in sowing and reaping, they need to repent for planting corn every spring for the last forty years so they could get more corn. They didn't sow those seeds because they just loved the ground and wanted to do something for the ground! They sowed seeds because they wanted to get something out of it for themselves. Besides, God showed us in His Word that He Himself has sown to reap. He sowed Jesus into the earth as a seed to reap us. God only had one Son, but He wanted more, so He sowed Jesus, and Jesus brought many sons with Him from the dead unto glory (Heb. 2:10).

Giving Connects the Natural With the Supernatural and Brings Supernatural Results

The reason we need to give in order to receive is, giving is an act of faith in the law of sowing and reaping. Giving connects the natural with the supernatural.

Every seed has a hull on the outside and meat on the inside. It's not really the hull of that seed that has the power in it to do anything. The hull or shell is actually just a container for the power that is inside. When it comes to planting faith and financial seed for financial needs in our lives, it is much the same way. The financial gift is really not the power that brings forth the supernatural. The gift is just the container that holds the faith which releases the anointing of God into that problem and destroys it. So if you want to release the power of God into a financial problem, plant a seed of faith. The gift is only the vehicle that you use to direct the power of God into a specific situation. Every seed produces after its own kind. If you want a car harvest, sow into someone else who needs a car. If you need clothes, sow clothes into someone's life.

It's amazing how a rose bulb can be planted in a plot of

soil and produce sweet-smelling flowers, but a chili plant can be planted in that some plot of ground and produce chilies so hot you can't bite into one without crying. What that means is that seeds will draw to themselves what they need to produce after their own kind. One seed draws sweet things to itself, and the other, bitter things. Glory to God! The same is true of seeds of faith. They'll draw to themselves whatever it takes to produce after their own kind. So if you need clothes, plant clothes! *Plant* whatever it is you need! And learn to plant professionally for a living. Ephesians 4:28 tells us to practice a *lifestyle* of giving toward needs and believing God, rather than working for things. God isn't telling us in this passage to *give*; He's telling us to *be a giver*. There is a difference.

How To Become a Professional Giver

Notice that Second Corinthians 9:7 said, "*. . . God loveth a cheerful GIVER.*" That doesn't include everyone. You may give at Christmas and Easter, but that doesn't make you a giver. You may give when you feel like it, but that doesn't make you a giver. A giver is someone who *practices* giving professionally on a regular basis for income. They give every chance they get, and they do it for a living.

How does a farmer become a farmer. Or, why do we call people lawyers, bankers, plumbers, writers, and so forth? Because they do those things professionally for a living. Just because I built a doghouse one time doesn't make me a builder. Or just because I balance my checkbook doesn't make me a banker. A person becomes a builder or banker because they do the things it takes to be in those positions professionally on a regular basis. They do them for a living. Some of them study for years in order to be a professional in their particular area.

That's what the Bible means when it tells us to become givers. We ought to take the time to meditate in the Word of God along this line and become skilled in giving for a living. As a painter seeks out opportunities to paint for income, you and I are to seek out opportunities to give for income. Once you understand that, you'll not check to see if your income supports your lifestyle, you'll check to see if your *giving* supports your lifestyle. You'll understand that your giving sets your prosperity and not your income, in much the same way that a thermostat sets the temperature of a room and not the thermometer. The thermometer eventually records what the thermostat is set at, but it isn't what *controls* the room temperature. Similarly, God doesn't want your paycheck to control you — He wants it to be a tool to raise the temperature of your prosperity!

It would do your mentality a lot of good to begin to tell people that you are a giver when they ask you what you do for a living. The first thing doing that will do is get your mind renewed, and, second, talking about giving will keep you conscious of the fact that you are not limited by that job you work at. Your constant confession will keep your faith active for the best that God has for you.

Begin sowing toward needs you may have. Make up your mind you're not going to get lazy spiritually, "flesh out," and just go buy things on a credit card. Decide that if your faith doesn't get those things for you, then you're not going to have them.

If You Have Money, God Wants You To Have *More*

This will also work for people who have the money in the bank to buy what they need. This "seed faith" I'm talking about is for rich people too. We're not supposed to bail out of financial problems by faith, we're supposed to *live* by faith. It would do people who have money a lot of good spiritually to give some money away to someone who needs what they need. Then they should believe God to supply their own need, rather than just supplying it themselves.

We are never to be dependent on our bank account to provide our needs. Giving what we have in the bank away is a good way to get our dependence back on God. Now I know that some people will think that is extreme, but that's the reason they aren't loaded with money. If you want the best God has for you, you need to keep your faith in Him.

God will meet you at your point of faith no matter if you are at the top of the barrel or the bottom financially. The important thing is not where you are, but that you have faith in and trust God.

In fact, there was a king in the Old Testament who got in trouble with God because he hired an army to fight his battles and didn't trust God to deliver him out of the hands of his enemies (2 Chron. 25:1-9). He just bought his way out of a problem and didn't put his faith in God. God wants our faith to be in Him, and it doesn't matter to him whether we have money in the bank or not. He wants us to do things His way even when we don't have to. *That* is excellence, and God is pleased by it.

Give as a Lifestyle
To Receive as a Lifestyle

Many people's favorite verse concerning prosperity is Philippians 4:19, which says, "*But my God shall supply all your need according to his riches in glory by Christ Jesus.*" The word translated "supply" is the Greek word "pleroo" and it means *to make replete*; *to cram full*; *to level up*; *to satisfy*. The word translated "supply" is the same Greek word translated "filled" in Ephesians 5:18.

EPHESIANS 5:18
18 And be not drunk with wine, wherein is excess; but be filled with the Spirit.

Many of us know that this Greek word for "filled" has a play on it, and, literally, the word means to be being filled continuously. The same is true concerning the Lord's supplying all our needs! We could literally translate Philippians 4:19 to read, "But my God shall supply and continually resupply all your need over and over again according to His riches in glory by Christ Jesus"!

Glory to God! That's good, isn't it? We may all shout about that, but the truth is we don't all qualify for that blessing. "But, Brother Jay, isn't the Word of God for everyone"? Yes, and the blessing of Philippians 4:19 is for everyone who does what these Philippians did to get the blessing.

Notice something that Paul said to the Philippians concerning their giving before he ever told them that God would supply their needs over and over again.

PHILIPPIANS 4:15-17
15 Now ye Philippians know also, that in the beginning of the gospel, when I departed from Macedonia,

no church communicated with me as concerning giving and receiving, but ye only.
16 For even in Thessalonica ye sent ONCE AND AGAIN unto my necessity.
17 Not because I desire a gift: but I desire FRUIT THAT MAY ABOUND TO YOUR ACCOUNT.

Did you see why Paul said that God would be the Philippians' constant source of provision? It was because they gave "once and again." In other words, they didn't just send Paul an offering a time or two to help him preach the Gospel. No, they were giving on a constant basis. They were giving professionally, for a living. In fact, we see from the beginning of the Book of Philippians that they had become partners with Paul's ministry (Phil. 1:3-7).

If you and I want to make a living by our giving, then we're going to have to practice giving on a regular basis. One thing about sowing seeds of faith financially is that you don't have to wait till the fall of every year to reap a harvest. Harvesttime can be year-round if you practice sowing year-round. I don't want long periods of time to go by before another financial harvest comes in, do you?

Chapter 9
Partners in the Gospel

We saw in the last chapter that the Philippians were partners in Paul's ministry. Let's look closer at the Philippians' relationship to his ministry.

PHILIPPIANS 1:3-7
3 I thank my God upon every remembrance of you,
4 Always in every prayer of mine for you all making request with joy,
5 For your FELLOWSHIP IN THE GOSPEL FROM THE FIRST DAY UNTIL NOW;
6 Being confident of this very thing, that he which hath begun a good work in you will perform it until the day of Jesus Christ:
7 Even as it is meet for me to think this of you all, because I have you in my heart; inasmuch as both in my bonds, and in the defence and confirmation of the gospel, YE ARE ALL PARTAKERS OF MY GRACE.

To the casual reader of the Bible, these verses don't seem to have any connection to Paul's comments in the fourth chapter of Philippians, but they actually reveal much about their partnership together in the Gospel. Notice some other translations of verse 5:

The *Rotherham* translation says that Paul was thankful on account of their *"contribution unto the glad message."*

The *Revised Standard Version* said that Paul was thankful for their *"partnership in the gospel."*

The Amplified Bible says, "[I thank my God] for your fellowship — your sympathetic cooperation and contributions and partnership — in advancing the good news (the Gospel) from the first day [you heard it] until now." Notice in particular that it said Paul thanked God for their contributions, *plural.*

The word "fellowship" in this verse means "sharing." Once again, Paul makes mention of the fact that they had shared of their material blessings with him over and over again from the very time they got saved. In other words, they were living a lifestyle of giving to the Gospel. They were using their money to help spread the message that set them free.

There Is Divine Order in Financial Prosperity

This is the divine order. When we are fed the Word of God, we are to support our teachers in their work by paying them (Gal. 6:6). The Bible says that if someone sows spiritual things into our lives, they should reap our carnal things (1 Cor. 9:11). By doing so, we become fellow helpers to the truth (3 John 8). You may not go and preach the Gospel all over the world, but you sure can use your money to send someone else. All of us should either be go-ers, senders, or prayers. Just because you don't have a call into the full-time ministry doesn't mean that you can't have a part in preaching the Gospel. Your money can send the Gospel message around the world.

We need to think "teamwork" in getting people to God. Psalm 68:11 says, *"The Lord gave the word: great was the company of those that published it."*

The Lord Himself had partners who supported His ministry on a regular basis from start to finish.

LUKE 8:1-3
1 And it came to pass afterward, that he went throughout every city and village, preaching and shewing the glad tidings of the kingdom of God: and the twelve were with him,
2 And certain women, which had been healed of evil spirits and infirmities, Mary called Magdalene, out of whom went seven devils,
3 And Joanna the wife of Chuza Herod's steward, and Susanna, and MANY OTHERS, WHICH MINISTERED UNTO HIM OF THEIR SUBSTANCE.

These people were helping Jesus' ministry by giving into it. It's interesting that those who gave were people who had been ministered to by Jesus' ministry. Some had been delivered of devils and cured of ailments. I'm sure that some of these women who are mentioned were quite wealthy and gave sizable offerings because of who the Bible says they were. One lady was the wife of the treasurer of the entire nation. Susanna was Zebedee's wife. We know from the scriptures that Zebedee had a good-sized fishing business.

It says that there were many others besides those who are mentioned. Glory to God! Jesus, I'm sure, believed God for them, and if He did, you know His faith worked and worked *big*.

God is actively looking for partners who will join with Him in what He is doing in the earth so that He can get involved in what they are doing.

What It Means To Be in Partnership

A partnership according to the English dictionary is an association of two or more people for the purpose of some business endeavor or undertaking in which each furnishes labor or capitol and are entitled to a certain part of the profits or losses according to what proportion is invested.

In other words, giving into the Gospel is like a business relationship. When we regularly support a work of God that God has used in our lives, God sees it as a business relationship.

God doesn't need people to give in order to take care of His ministers. He has proven that by causing ravens to bring bread to the prophet Elijah. He has been known to cause water to come out of a rock in the wilderness, bring manna out of the sky, and send angels to cook a meal for one of His servants. But He would rather use *people* to bless His ministers, because He wants to get the blessing that is on that minister onto someone else, not just once, but over and over again. He wants to be in partnership with people. Partnership in not just a one-sided thing. Many people see partnership as a ministry getting an offering on a regular basis, but there is much more to it than that.

Did you notice what Paul said to his partners at Philippi in Philippians 1:7? The very last statement in that verse says, *"...ye all are partakers of my grace."* In other words, Paul was telling them that anything that came on him from God was going to come on them as well, because they were his partners.

I like that, don't you? When you're in partnership, each party is entitled to the profits, because each is putting something into it.

As I said, partnership is not a one-sided thing. God intends to bless you in return for what you give into a partnership.

There are some excellent examples of partnership in the Old Testament. Let's notice some of them.

God Uses Partnerships To Sustain You, Meet Your Need, and Prosper You

The first one is found in First Kings 17:1-24. It's the story of Elijah prophesying about a drought that was coming to the nation of Israel. God fed him supernaturally for a while by causing ravens to bring food to him. But soon, the brook he was drinking from dried up. Then God spoke to him to go to Zarephath because he had commanded a widow woman there to sustain him.

When Elijah got to the city, he found the woman and asked her for some water to drink. As she went to get the water he said, "*. . . Bring me, I pray thee, a morsel of bread in thine hand*" (1 Kings 17:11).

The woman answered him, "*. . . As the Lord thy God liveth, I have not a cake, but an handful of meal in a barrel, and a little oil in a cruse: and, behold, I am gathering two sticks, that I may go in and dress it for me and my son, that we may eat it, and die*" (v. 12).

Elijah said, "*. . . Fear not; go and do as thou hast said: but make me thereof a little cake first, and bring it unto me, and after make for thee and for thy son. For thus saith the Lord God of Israel, The barrel of meal shall not waste, neither shall the cruse of oil fail, until the day that the Lord sendeth rain upon the earth*" (vv. 13,14).

Notice the result.

1 KINGS 17:15
15 And she went and did according to the saying of Elijah: and she, and he, and her house, did eat many days.

You see, God needed to get a blessing on a man of God, so He called someone into partnership with Him. Notice that he used a very unlikely person to do it. The reason He did was, she needed to be in partnership with someone as bad as Elijah needed a partnership. You would think that God would send Elijah to a rich person's house in order to take care of him until the famine was over. But God doesn't do things the way we do. God looks for faith more than resources — someone who has money. If He can find someone who has faith, He can bless him at the same time He blessed the one he's in partnership with.

Jesus said in Luke 4:24-26 that there were many widows in Israel at the time Elijah needed a partnership. From the context of Jesus' words, we know that Elijah was sent to this particular widow because of her faith. It took faith to give Elijah the last morsel of food that she had in her house. Giving up her last morsel seemed like a foolish thing to do, but, thank God, because of her faith in the word from God, it turned out to be the wisest thing she ever did. She ended up eating well during the entire famine. Her prosperity came from being in partnership with someone whom God had spoken to her to support.

That's not the end of the story, either.

When her son later died, as recorded in the very next verses, she supernaturally received him back to life again. That sure was a blessing, wasn't it? Notice who God used to get this blessing to her. It was the ministry that she was in partnership with.

Supernatural Contacts

I believe that if we will listen to God, He will give us supernatural contacts with the right people so that when we get into a hard place in life, we'll be in partnership with someone whom God can use to help us out. I know that some people don't realize that God wants to use others to get the blessing to them, but that's just the way He does things. We are the Body of Christ.

Your arm gets its supply of blood, nerve impulses, and so forth, from other members of your body. The instructions that your brain gives don't go through the air to your arm, do they? No, they come through the nerves in your neck and shoulder. Your arm wouldn't function very well if it weren't connected where it was supposed to be.

The same is true with the Body of Christ. We were never meant to be "lone rangers" out there all by ourselves. We're supposed to be hooked up somewhere. Where God hooks us up is where our supply is going to come from, whether we are a church member or a minister (Eph. 4:16). If you decide not to show up anymore at the church the Lord put you in, then the instructions you need to prosper will never fully reach you, just like your arm wouldn't get what it needs if it decided not to stay hooked up to the shoulder. We all need our "own company" to go to in the time of need (Acts 4:23). If we don't stay hooked up where we belong, we'll cut ourselves off from our supply.

This is particularly true concerning the local church that God put you in. Many times, we only think of being partners with missionaries or traveling evangelists, but you can become a partner with your local church. If you don't stay hooked up to your local church through your tithes and offerings, your lack of faithfulness to the principle of partnership will cut you off from the spiritual deposits that you need.

Give Honor Those to Whom Honor Is Due

Why do I say that? The Bible says, *"Let the elders that rule well be counted worthy of double honour, especially they who labour in the word and doctrine. For the scripture saith, Thou shalt not muzzle the ox that treadeth out the corn. And, The labourer is worthy of his reward"* (1 Tim. 5:17,18).

According to these two verses, if we don't support the ministry with our money, it muzzles the mouth of the one who is working for us spiritually. The two main things that we do with our mouth is eat and speak. In First Timothy 5, Paul is certainly referring to the fact that a minister is to make his living by the tithes and offerings of the people. But, another way you could interpret this verse would be to say that when we *don't* support those who minister to us, it keeps that ministry from having utterance in the Holy Ghost to speak into our lives. A muzzle goes over the mouth, doesn't it? If we keep a minister poor whom God has hooked us up with by not partnering with him, it keeps that ministry from operating on our behalf.

I like all the help I can get when hard times come, so I make sure not to muzzle the mouth of those whom God has used to speak into my life.

Paul talks further about these things in First Corinthians 9:7-11.

1 CORINTHIANS 9:7-11
7 Who goeth a warfare any time at his own charges?

who planteth a vineyard, and eateth not of the fruit thereof? or WHO FEEDETH A FLOCK, AND EATETH NOT THE MILK OF THE FLOCK?
8 Say I these things as a man? or saith not the law the same also?
9 For it is written in the law of Moses, THOU SHALT NOT MUZZLE THE MOUTH OF THE OX THAT TREADETH OUT THE CORN. Doth God take care for oxen?
10 Or saith he it altogether for our sakes? For our sakes, no doubt, this is written: that he that ploweth should plow in hope; and that he that thresheth in hope should be partaker of his hope.
11 IF WE HAVE SOWN UNTO SPIRITUAL THINGS, IS IT A GREAT THING IF WE SHALL REAP YOUR CARNAL THING?

There was a time in my life when I first went into ministry that I meditated on this passage of Scripture quite often in order to establish it in my spirit. I'll never forget during one of those seasons of meditation how the Lord spoke to me in a night vision. I am satisfied that the Lord has only spoken to me four or five times in this manner, but it is scriptural (Acts 16:9).

I grew up on a farm and am very familiar with cattle and their needs. In the night vision I saw a hired hand on my father's farm lead a cow into what we called a box stall, which is simply a square stall for tending to a cow in some particular way. In this situation, the cow was ready to give birth to a calf.

As I observed the hired man in my vision, he assisted the cow in giving birth by pulling on the calf's front legs as it came out, which is a normal practice. Once the calf was born, the man left and went to tend to other business without making sure the calf's mouth and nose were clear of mucus so it could breathe. Nor did he assist the calf in finding its mothers milk, which is very important to both the cow and calf once the calf is born.

A while later, the hired hand came to check on the cow and calf only to find that they had both died. To my utter amazement (in fact, it woke me up from my dream), I whirled the hired man around and kicked him in the seat of the pants!

As I lay there in the bed thinking on what I had just seen, I remembered how there had been times on the farm growing up that we had lost cows after they had given birth because of a disease called milk fever. Milk fever will cause a cow to die within minutes or at the most a few hours if the condition isn't treated immediately. A cow can get milk fever if it isn't relieved of the right amounts of milk at the right times.

Don't Let the Supply of Your Finances Dry Up!

I'll never forget what the Lord said to me that early morning after I'd had that vision. He took me back to this passage we just read and quoted the part to me that says, *"... who feedeth a flock, and eateth not the milk of the flock?"* (1 Cor. 9:7). Then He said something to me I'll never forget. He said, "If the ministry doesn't draw off of the people, the people's finances will dry up and die." I almost didn't know for sure if I was hearing right. I said, "Lord, that's pretty bold. Do You really want me to tell people that?"

Pondering the vision in which both the cow and the calf died, I realized that the Holy Ghost was speaking to me so that I wouldn't be backward about receiving offerings, but there is another side to what God was saying to me. People also need to know that if they don't take care of their ministers, it will kill their own financial blessings, because they "killed" the man's ministry that God was using to get that blessing to them.

We all know that a newborn calf needs to eat in order to stay alive, but few people know that a cow needs to *give* in order to keep producing milk and, in some cases, to stay alive. In the same way, if people don't support their ministers financially, it can kill their own financial blessings, because they killed the ministry that God was using to get that blessing to them.

When I went back to this passage of Scripture in First Corinthians and read the whole thing again, sure enough, there was this verse about the muzzle. As I meditated on the passage further, I noticed it said that if we receive spiritual things, we are to minister our carnal things to the one who is feeding us. In other words, if we don't minister our natural things to those who are feeding us spiritually, the spiritual things will dry up and cause our financial blessing to dry up as well. I remember on the farm that if we quit milking a cow, that cow would eventually stop producing milk.

Did you notice that the widow woman we read about in First Kings 17 continued to feed Elijah throughout the entire famine and also had a continual supply of blessings as long as she took care of her partner? If she would have gotten offended at Elijah half way through the famine and kicked him out for eating half her food, she would have kicked her blessing out the door as well.

God took care of another woman through her partnership with the prophet Elisha (who was Elijah's contemporary) in Second Kings 4:8-37. There we find the story of the great woman of Shunem. She and her husband built an addition onto their house in order to bless the man of God and, by doing so, went into a business relationship with God.

The Benefits of Faithful Partnership Are Ongoing

The Shunammite took care of the man of God and in return received a son from the Lord. When her son later died, God used the man she was in partnership with to raise him from the dead. Then in Second Kings chapter 8, God told Elisha to tell the woman and her husband that a famine was coming to their land and that they should move away until it was over. I like that, don't you? God told them what the economy was going to do and what to do about it. Glory to God! But that's not the end of the story.

After the famine was over, the woman returned to her land only to find that someone had moved into her house and "set up shop." They didn't have laws like we have today, so she had to go see where she could find help. She went all the way to the king before she got help. Even then, the only reason she received help was because it "just so happened" that when she walked in, the king was talking to Elisha's servant about how Elisha had raised a widow woman's son from the dead!

2 KINGS 8:5,6
5 And it came to pass, as he [Gehazi, Elisha's servant] **was telling the king how he** [Elisha] **had restored a dead body to life, that, behold, the woman, whose son he had restored to life, cried to the king for her house and for her land. And Gehazi said, My lord, O king,**

this is the woman, and this is her son, whom Elisha restored to life.
6 And when the king asked the woman, she told him. So the king appointed unto her a certain officer, saying, Restore all that was hers, and all the fruits of the field since the day that she left the land, even until now.

The real reason she got all her land back with all the crops it had produced was, she came in contact with the partnership that she had formed earlier with Elisha. There is no reason to believe that there were any laws that required the king to do anything for her.

Can you see the power of partnership? Partnership isn't a one-sided thing. This woman was continuing to be blessed in the things of God seven years after she formed her partnership with Elisha.

You may not be doing what the ministry is doing that you're in partnership with, but you've invested into that ministry, so anything that comes on your partner comes on you, too, because you've been working together with that person or ministry. It's all the same thing in God's eyes.

Direct Your Giving Toward the Anointing

You need to go into partnership with someone who has something on him or her to partake of. Don't support some church that isn't even preaching the New Birth. You even need to be careful not to support something who isn't feeding you spiritually. If he preaches from the *Reader's Digest*, there is not much blessing there, and there certainly isn't going to be any anointing on it.

Direct your giving toward the anointing. You need to know who you're giving to. It's the anointing that destroys the yoke (Isa. 10:27). If you're sowing seed into the anointing, you'll get that anointing on you because of your association with that ministry. Jesus said there are different rewards for different ministries (Matt. 10:40-42), so understand and esteem the value of partnerships, because they will play a big part in your financial prosperity and blessing.

Chapter 10

The Roles of Faith and Miracles in Prosperity

We have seen in earlier chapters that God told his Old Testament people He was giving them power to obtain wealth. The Bible also called this "empowering to prosper" the *blessing*.

We have seen that a key to receiving this blessing is to walk in God's ways.

> **PSALM 1:1-3**
> **1 BLESSED is the man that walketh not in the counsel of the ungodly, nor standeth in the way of sinners, nor sitteth in the seat of the scornful.**
> **2 BUT HIS DELIGHT IS IN THE LAW OF THE LORD; and in his law doth he meditate day and night.**
> **3 And he shall be like a tree planted by the rivers of water, that bringeth forth his fruit in his season; his leaf also shall not wither; and whatsoever he doeth shall PROSPER.**

Furthermore, we have learned that God's way of prospering us is through our operating on His heavenly banking system. Through laying up treasures in Heaven and believing God for a return, we can expect to supersede any of man's ways of increasing financially.

God desires for us to come into a business relationship with Him so that He can bring His power on the scene in our financial dealings!

Learn That Money Is a Tool

Money is simply an "envelope" that we use to wrap our faith in and then use in order to plant the power of God into a need. Money is not the power to provide the need; it is a vehicle to release our faith. We can learn to plant or sow professionally, for a living. As we do, all the limits on how prosperous we can be will be removed, because we've tapped into the supernatural. What a thought!

One of the keys to understanding how to tap into supernatural prosperity is to learn how to recognize when God is moving by His Spirit and to sow into it.

Many times we have heard people say that we need to be sure to plant our seed into good ground. Have you ever asked yourself the question, "What makes a ministry good ground?" Certainly, good ground would be ground that will multiply your seed the most. But the next question is, "What is it that actually multiplies the seed?"

In order to answer that question, we must realize that God multiplied seed two different ways in the Bible. He multiplied seed simply by *faith*, which means that when people acted in faith on the simple law of sowing and reaping, their seed multiplied according to their faith.

On the other hand, God has multiplied seed in the Bible by *the manifestation of the gifts of the Spirit.*

Just as we see people being healed by faith, we also see people receiving financial provision by their faith. On the other side of the coin, we see people healed as well as receiving provision by one of the gifts of the Spirit in operation.

When we sow our seed in obedience to the simple law of sowing and reaping, our seed will multiply according to the faith that we sow with as well as the faith that is in the ground we sowed into. On the other hand, when we sow seed while a manifestation of one of the gifts of the Spirit is in manifestation, we can realize a return that far surpasses our faith.

Not only do we see that the Bible teaches the law of multiplication, but we see that it teaches that there are *miracles* of multiplication.

One passage that has taught me much along this line is found in Matthew 14.

MATTHEW 14:15-21
15 And when it was evening, his [Jesus'] **disciples came to him, saying, This is a desert place, and the time is now past; send the multitude away, that they may go into the villages, and buy themselves victuals.**
16 But Jesus said unto them, They need not depart; give ye them to eat.
17 And they say unto him, We have here but five loaves, and two fishes.
18 He said, Bring them hither to me.
19 And he commanded the multitude to sit down on the grass, and took the five loaves, and the two fishes, and looking up to heaven, he blessed, and brake, and gave the loaves to his disciples, and the disciples to the multitude.
20 And they did all eat, and were filled: and they took up of the fragments that remained twelve baskets full.
21 And they that had eaten were about five thousand men, beside women and children.

I think this must be the greatest multiplication of a seed that we have record of in the Scriptures. A little boy gave his lunch to Jesus which ended up feeding at least 15,000 people! There were

5,000 men there, so we can safely say that there were 5,000 women and at least 5,000 children there, if not more. If that little boy's lunch was enough to feed one man, then he sowed a seed that multiplied 15,000 times in one afternoon!

Someone said, "Now, Brother Jay, you know that isn't going to happen for anybody."

It's not a matter of whether it's ever going to happen; it's a matter of it already happening! It already happened to a little boy. The Bible said so.

"Well," someone else said, "the loaves were bigger in those days, and it probably wasn't really that much of a miracle."

But if that "big" loaf fed 15,000 people, that little boy would have had to carry that giant loaf on a tractor trailer to that meeting! (Some people want to doubt everything they find in the Bible.)

Uncommon Multiplication

This Bible account in many ways parallels the way things work in our lives. There was a need, but what the little boy had wasn't enough to meet the need. Many people come upon situations like this one on a regular basis and don't get this kind of miracle. What was different about this particular situation? What was it about this seed that caused it to multiply so much?

First, we need to understand that there is a Godward side and a manward side to everything. This is certainly true concerning the feeding of the five thousand. In this case, we need to understand that Jesus had a manifestation of working of miracles in operation. That is the Godward side. On the other side, the little boy obeyed the Lord and gave his lunch to Him when He asked for it. We need to spend time looking at both sides in order to fully understand how such a large multiplication of this seed came about in one afternoon.

I believe we are living in a day in which there is a special move of God in the earth that is bringing these kinds of financial miracles back into operation in a greater measure. We're living in a day in which the Body of Christ is being equipped with more than the simple laws of sowing and reaping, which works by ordinary faith.

Certainly, God expects the Church to continue to sow their seed in faith, because the just shall live by faith. But we're living in a day in which the working of miracles is beginning to operate to bring about the uncommon — unusual multiplication of seeds sown. I, for one, am very excited about it! This operation of the Spirit is what it is going to take to bring about the transfer of the wealth of the wicked into the hands of the just.

I have thought many times that we need to rightly divide the Word of God when it comes to these kinds of returns. We can't necessarily promise people that they'll receive the kind of return we just read about in Matthew 14 on every seed they sow. Certainly, if they can believe God for it, God can do it. But people need to be honest with themselves and realize that they aren't at the place where they can believe for a 15,000-fold return on every seed sown! It takes the manifestation of the working of miracles in operation in order to manifest these kinds of results.

It's very similar to the fact that some have thought they could raise people from the dead by faith. You can't just raise anyone from the dead anytime you want to by faith. It takes the operation of several of the gifts of the Spirit. If you could do it by faith, you would be doing it all the time.

It's time the Body of Christ learns to recognize the difference between the *spiritual law* of multiplication and the *miracle* of multiplication. We have recognized the difference between someone being healed by their faith as opposed to his being healed by one of the gifts of the Spirit, such as working of miracles or the gift of special faith. However, we haven't fully recognized the difference between receiving prosperity by sowing seeds in faith versus by the working of miracles or the gift of special faith coming into operation.

There are basically two different ways that God moves. He moves by our faith, but He also moves by the gifts of the Spirit. When it comes to the account of the feeding of the five thousand, God moved by the manifestation of the gift of the Spirit called working of miracles.

Miracles of Provision

We also need to understand that there are different kinds of miracles.

HEBREWS 2:4
4 God also bearing them witness, both with signs and wonders, and with DIVERS miracles, and gifts of the Holy Ghost, according to his own will.

The word translated "divers" in the *King James Version* of the Bible means *various in character.* You can readily see from the Scriptures that there are miracles of *healing*, miracles of *nature* (the splitting of the Red Sea and so forth), and miracles of *provision*.

The Church has already begun to see the working of miracles coming into operation in a greater way to provide for the people of God. (I tell you by the Spirit of God that it has already begun.) We need to continue to sow seed as we have purposed in our heart and to use our faith as we have been doing, because, as I said before, the just shall live by faith.

But we need to recognize and be aware of the fact that God is wanting to do some extra things in our day. He's wanting to transfer the wealth of the sinner into the hands of the just. If you continue to sow by faith (as you have purposed in your heart) and believe for a harvest, you are being counted as one of the faithful ones who can handle the transfer of huge amounts of wealth that are on their way to you.

There is something very interesting about the feeding of the five thousand in Matthew chapter 14. In this case, the little boy didn't offer his lunch (seed) to Jesus. The Bible says Jesus *asked* for it.

MATTHEW 14:17,18
17 And they say unto him, We have here but five loaves, and two fishes.
18 He said, Bring them hither to me.

The Bible teaches us that every man is to give according as he purposes in his heart (1 Cor. 9:7; Exod. 35-36). If that is so, then why did Jesus tell the disciples to go get the little boy's lunch and bring it to Him? Because there was more happening there than the simple law of sowing and reaping, which works by faith.

When we use our faith for prosperity, we initiate the supernatural by our giving. When the gift of working of miracles is in manifestation, we have to do something, but we don't initiate the action. God initiates the action by giving us a command to do something.

Notice it is called the *"working"* of miracles. When this gift is in manifestation, we are equipped by the Holy Ghost to "work" the miracle, but we can only do it because the anointing of the Holy Ghost comes upon us in that instant to do so. Certainly, without the anointing we wouldn't be able to do anything. Without the anointing on Moses, for example, he wouldn't have been able to split the Red Sea by simply holding out his rod. But, thank God, when the anointing is on you and you obey what God told you to do, you work the miracle.

Miracles Require Action on Our Part

In Acts 8:5 and 6, the Bible tells us that the people of Samaria gave heed to Philip's preaching the Gospel, "hearing and seeing the miracles which he did." Miracles require action on our part.

When Jesus turned the water into wine in John chapter 2, that certainly was a miracle, wasn't it? Mary gave us the key to miracles when she told the servants, "Whatever He saith unto you, *do it*!" When they obeyed Jesus' instructions to fill the water pots with water and carry them to the governor of the feast, they worked a miracle.

If you study closely the account of Jesus feeding the five thousand, there is no faith displayed on the part of the disciples, the multitude, or the little boy. The only thing we see is obedience. Certainly, there is an element of faith in obedience, but if you study the subject of faith carefully, you'll find that when faith is in operation, it initiates the power of God. In this case, no one stepped out in faith and initiated this miracle. Jesus initiated it by giving the instructions to go get the little boy's lunch.

If you'll take the time to think about the working of miracles, you'll discover that it really does involve faith to manifest it, because you have to step out and do something as a result of what God tells you to do. However, when that anointing lifts from you, and you are back to using your own faith that comes by hearing the written Word of God (Rom. 10:17), you can't produce the same results that you were able to produce when you had the manifestation of the Spirit.

When it comes to financial miracles as we see in the case of the feeding of the five thousand, you work the miracle by giving what the Lord speaks to you to give. As a result, you will get uncommon, extraordinary results that you can't always get by simply sowing your seed when there is no manifestation of the Spirit in operation. When you have no special leading to give or there is no anointing on you to give, that doesn't mean that sowing in faith won't work. You can purpose in your heart to give and reap a harvest on your seed by faith.

For example, a farmer doesn't need any special direction from God or a special anointing in manifestation in order to reap a crop. He can just decide how many acres of seed to plant and then reap according to how much he planted.

My point is that you need to recognize and be aware of the fact that when the anointing comes on you and the Lord tells you to sow a certain amount of money in a certain place, you are being set up for an unusual miracle of multiplication. I'm not talking about some preacher pumping up a crowd's emotions until they'll do anything he tells them to. I'm talking about when the anointing gets in the chair with you and tells you to do something.

When you understand these things, you'll understand that Elijah had the anointing on him to tell the widow woman in First Kings 17:8-16 to make him a little cake first before she made one for her baby and herself. He had the manifestation of the working of miracles. The widow must have sensed the anointing or she never would have obeyed. Personally, I wouldn't do something just because someone says I should. There is a tremendous amount of danger in doing that. Some Christians aren't spiritually mature enough to know the real move of the Spirit from the false, and they are easily taken in by covetous men who don't know God and who have lost the anointing. Many Christians are so hungry for the move of God that they will do anything a ministers tells them to do.

In the Bible, you don't see any minister more than one

or two times in the course of his ministry instruct someone to give something to him as Elijah did. I believe the statistics should be the same today. A minister is in error who is telling people all the time "I'm anointed. Give your money to me and you'll get your miracle." If a minister is anointed, the people will know it, and God will tell them what to do without the minister's "help."

Don't misunderstand me. It's not wrong for a minister to tell people what his ministry is doing and to encourage them to sow seed when it comes time to take up the offering. Any minister who doesn't believe his ministry is good ground ought to get out of the ministry. My point is, let's let God be God. Let's let God deal with people about what to do.

Besides, it's not always necessary to *give* in order to experience financial miracles. We see that the water was turned into wine simply by filling the water pots with water. Peter experienced a miracle when he threw a hook in the lake and caught a fish with money in its mouth to pay his taxes. In this case, he just did what the Lord told him to do.

Let's just stay scriptural about these things. Giving is involved in the working of miracles, but not on every occasion. Let's just let God be God and enjoy the blessings that are coming our way!

When the Lord does speak to us to give, we should realize that by giving, we're releasing our miracle. When we sow into that kind of anointing, we reap that anointing in return. It is the anointing that multiplies the seed, breaks the yoke, and meets the need!

We need to realize the day we live in. You will begin to be in more and more services in which God will move in a special way in order to bring financial miracles to His people. You need to be aware of the times during which He is moving and jump in. How do you do that? Simply by doing whatever He says to do.

You see, the miracle isn't in what you *don't* have; it's in what you *do* have. God needs something to get started with. All He really needs is for you to obey and sow what you have.

Notice a few things that the little boy did differently than people who don't experience miracles. As we said, there is a manward side to the supernatural as well as a Godward side.

First of all, the little boy didn't discredit the small amount that he had, as the disciples did. Notice what the disciples said about the little boy's lunch: "*. . . We have here but five loaves, and two fishes*" (Luke 14:17). In other words, they were saying, "We only have a little bit of food.

Direct Your Money Toward The Work of God, Not Toward Needs

The second thing the little boy did that was different than others who don't experience the miracle of multiplication is, he didn't direct the loaves and the fishes toward the need. He gave it to Jesus.

Notice that the people had the need, but the little boy didn't give the food to the people. He gave it to Jesus. When people have needs, many will hold on to everything they have until the need is met. If this little boy had done that, he wouldn't have had enough to feed even one other little boy in the crowd that day, and he certainly wouldn't have taken those twelve baskets of bread and fish home to his mother.

Can you see how people miss the miracle of multiplication? They direct their money toward needs instead of toward the anointing. As I said, it is the anointing that multiplies the seed, breaks the yoke, and meets the need!

It will be to your benefit in all areas of your life to attend a local church that believes and preaches prosperity and allows the Spirit of God to move in this area. Every believer needs a local church that he can call home. First, he needs to take his tithes there and then begin to sow seed into the church. This is where prosperity begins.

Your Prosperity Begins With Your Sowing Into Your Local Church

"But, Brother Jay, there just isn't a good church in my town."

Some people who say that just don't want to submit to the good one that is there. But if there really isn't a good one in your town, then move to a town where there is one!

"Well, we just can't do that. That would cost a lot of money."

Just stay poor and regretful then! If you are drying up spiritually where you are going to church, and you don't have any more tenacity than that, you never will get anywhere in the area of prosperity. I can tell you right now, it will cost you more money to stay in that dead church than it will to move to a good church where they believe and preach prosperity and where the Spirit of God is moving to bless and prosper people.

You need to be under the anointing on a regular basis, and you need to give your money where the anointing is in manifestation. One of the best places to sow is into your "own company" — into those of like-precious faith — because that is where your supply is. Ephesians 4:16 says that joints *supply*.

Where God has called you to join hands with other believers is where your supply is. If you are out of joint with the family that God has called you to fellowship with, you're not going to experience all the prosperity that God has for you to enjoy. The people you fellowship with should be full of faith for prosperity themselves.

Sow Your Money Into Those Who Have Faith for Prosperity

Find a church where the people have the faith and anointing on them to do more for God than they could ever possibly pay for and start supporting them with your faith by sowing into it.

When my wife and I look for a place to sow, we look for people of faith. As I said, you need not wait for the gifts of the Spirit to come into operation in order to reap a crop, because God multiplies seed two different ways — by our faith and by manifestations of the Spirit. Faith is for everyday living. To reap a good crop, just look around for some real good soil and sow your seed there. Then keep it watered by speaking the Word in faith over your seed.

The Bible tells us to give every time we have an opportunity, but especially to those who are of faith (Gal. 6:10). Some of the best soil you'll ever sow into will be faith ministries. When I say "faith ministry," I don't mean someone who has the word "faith" on a sign out front. I'm talking about someone who lives by faith.

Beware of Those Who Try To Make Man Their Source

If someone needs to be guaranteed a certain amount of money to come to your church to minister, he isn't living by faith. He's making your church his source instead of making God his source. For that reason, he isn't pleasing God, because without faith, it's impossible to please Him (Heb. 11:6). Since that minister is making your church his source, his ministry has become bad soil, because there is no faith for prosperity in his ministry. If you sow into it, there will be no faith or agreement there to multiply your seed.

If a minister can't come to a church unless he is guaranteed a certain amount of money, he is operating his ministry beyond his level of faith and has gotten into sin. Romans 14:23 says *"...for whatsoever is not of faith is sin."* The Bible also calls unbelief evil (Num. 13:32). Since that is the case, an unbelieving ministry certainly isn't a good place to sow your seed.

My wife and I look for people to give to whom we believe God's blessing is on and who are growing in their ministry. We look for those people in much the same way investors look for companies who are well positioned to experience huge growth in the business world.

A ministry or church that continues to step out in faith by the leading of the Lord is keeping itself in position for continual growth. A ministry that continues to obey God will experience a continual increase in the anointing.

My wife and I look for people to give to who have demonstrated that they will step out in faith when God tells them to do something and who will stay put in the hard places. As a partner with those kinds of ministries, we are entitled to our share of the same kind of spiritual and financial increase that comes to their ministry.

If the ministry that you are supporting doesn't step out in faith when God tells its leaders to give or when God tells them to open a Bible school in Africa, for example, neither you nor that ministry is going to experience all the spiritual and natural growth that God has for you.

As I said, you especially want to sow into a ministry where the leaders use their faith in the area of prosperity. They should believe in the law of sowing and reaping — so much so, that they practice it for their own prosperity. Practicing the law of sowing and reaping will increase the multiplication ability of a ministry, because faith is what multiplies the seed.

How To Get in the Flow of Multiplied Blessings!

When Jesus received the little boy's seed — his lunch — in Matthew 14, He turned around and gave it to the disciples, and the disciples gave it to the people. The seed *kept being given* over and over again! It's easy to understand why the seed multiplied so many times when you realize that it multiplied each time it was given away. Each time someone got a piece of bread or fish, he broke some off for himself and passed the rest on to someone else in his company.

Let's read Mark's account in Mark chapter 6.

MARK 6:39-41
39 And he [Jesus] **commanded them to make all sit down BY COMPANIES upon the green grass.**
40 And they sat down in RANKS, BY HUNDREDS, AND BY FIFTIES.
41 And when he had taken the five loaves and the two fishes, he looked up to heaven, and blessed, and brake the loaves, and gave them to his disciples to set before them; and the two fishes divided he among them all.

I think you can easily see that Jesus had them sit down in companies so the disciples could give someone in each company a piece of bread. Then that person could, in turn, break off some bread and pass it on to someone else in his company. Each time they gave part of what they had received, it multiplied all over again. Glory to God!

The Lord said to me one day, "It's better to sow into a *sower* than into *soil*." I like that, don't you? Looking at things that way has helped me ever since.

Look for ministries to sow into that are reaching out to others in their giving and not just thinking of themselves. By sowing there, you will get a "twice-sown-seed" blessing!

For more product information from Jay Eberly Ministries, please write:

Jay Eberly Ministries
P.O. Box 614
Broken Arrow, Oklahoma 74013
or call
(918) 461-0789